Bitcoin Astrology

Other Books by Tim Bost

8 Billionaire Strategies for

Breakthrough Stock Market Success

Beyond The Shadows

Gann Secrets Revealed

Mercury, Money and the Markets

Surprising Alliances

The Big One

The Solar Eclipse of May 2012

The Solar Eclipse of October 2014

Bitcoin Astrology

edited by

Tim Bost

with contributions by

Bill Meridian

Gonçalo Moreira

Christeen Skinner

Wendy Stacey

Harmonic Research Associates

Palmetto, Florida, USA

Bitcoin Astrology

Submit all requests for reprinting to:

Harmonic Research Associates
611 Riviera Dunes Way, Unit 702
Palmetto, FL 34221 USA

The astrological and market charts in this publication were prepared with the Fibonacci/Galactic Trader software from PAS Inc. (www.galacticinvestor.com) and the Solar Fire, Solar Maps, and Nova Chartwheels programs available from Astrolabe (www.alabe.com). Other charts with permission as attributed throughout.

Published in the United States of America by Harmonic Research Associates.

www.HarmonicResearchAssociates.com

ISBN-10: 1-933198-64-8

ISBN-13: 978-1-933198-64-4

EAN: 9781933198644

Table of Contents

Introduction

There are genuine challenges in dealing with Bitcoin in a manner that maintains some semblance of sanity. After all, this pioneering cryptocurrency, along with its many progeny in the growing alt-coin family, has an uncanny knack for attracting hysteria.

The advocates for Bitcoin are vehemently enthusiastic, whether they envision it as a transformational force in the global economy or simply as a way to get very, very rich in a momentum-driven bubble.

Bitcoin detractors are often just as frenzied in their opposition. Whether they view it as a fraud, as a scam, or as an evil-intentioned scheme from a global conspiracy, they are quick to issue dire warnings to the uninformed. At the very least, they're ready at the drop of a hat with generous amounts of sarcasm and ridicule for those who are gullible enough to be duped by Bitcoin's promise of absolute privacy and ever-expanding wealth.

With such dedicated partisans on both sides of this often-heated conversation, the short history of Bitcoin has been extremely colorful thus far, to say the least.

It's true that Bitcoin has been the vehicle for the creation of a number of new millionaires. They were often the ones fortunate enough to have bought Bitcoin when its value was measured in pennies and then sell some of their holdings when Bitcoin was trading at tens of thousands of dollars.

In some cases they have used their new-found wealth to start new businesses, to pay off long-standing debts, to promote charitable causes, and along the way, to become even more vocal Bitcoin advocates.

It's also true that Bitcoin has created consternation for central banks and government regulators around the world. Its transformational potential for upsetting the global economic apple cart is certainly being taken seriously by the powers that be.

And yes, Bitcoin has been a key element in criminal activities and illicit enterprises. Some of its bedfellows have been particularly unsavory, and even dangerous to have as associates. Because of the ability to maintain privacy and conceal the amounts being transferred in discrete and unmediated person-to-person transactions, a digital wallet full of Bitcoin has in some situations become suspiciously synonymous with a suitcase full of cash.

So what's the real story?

Is Bitcoin the Next Big Thing, or is it something to be afraid of?

How do we go about making sense of it in a reasonable way, without getting sucked into the hysteria or being duped by the propaganda?

Whether Bitcoin ultimately proves to be the technological equivalent of the tulip bulb mania of the 1630s – or whether it is a harbinger of an egalitarian era of harmonious worldwide peer-to-peer cooperation – remains to be seen. But no matter what its long-term future looks like, in the present Bitcoin is clearly a dynamic, game-changing force that must be taken into account if we are to understand more fully the evolving social, commercial, technological, and geopolitical dynamics that are shaping our world.

That's where astrology comes in. Financial astrology is best understood as a branch of mundane astrology, the astrological craft that focuses on nations, on political processes, on the structures of large organizations, and on events with international consequences. In financial astrology we are concerned with markets, commercial activities, commodities, currencies, and the actions of individuals or regulatory bodies which either promote or retard the expansion of business and innovation.

Whether we are new students of the astrological craft or are professional astrologers with decades of experience, we have a shared responsibility for employing the best tools and knowledge at our disposal to provide the kind of insights and well-intentioned guidance that can truly be helpful to others as they try to cope with shifting economic realities, grapple with key decisions, and embark on creative enterprises and fresh innovations in their quest for a more fulfilling and prosperous life.

That sense of responsibility is what gave birth to this book. In putting it together, our aim has been to bring together some of today's best minds who have demonstrated high levels of integrity in carrying forward the time-honored tradition of astrology as a refined spiritual science.

At the same time, our goal has been to create a tool that will prove useful not only to astrologers today and tomorrow, but also to traders, investors, and speculators who want to add the astro-trading advantage to their engagement with Bitcoin.

The contributors to this volume have bought their considerable skill and experience in financial astrology and market analysis to contribute to our understanding of the implications and possibilities that Bitcoin presents, both in and out of the markets. They have come to this task as analysts, as counselors, and as educators, bringing diverse perspectives and an international flavor to the information they share.

They are all recognized experts, and the synergy created by their diversity adds value and strength to what this book has to offer. We are enormously grateful for their willingness to share their insights in these pages.

Christeen Skinner is eminently cognizant of the time-honored traditions of financial astrological analysis; she is keenly connected with its roots in mundane astrology. She has gained a much-deserved international reputation for her insightful and well-articulated presentations of long-term economic trends as seen from an astrological perspective.

Christeen also takes an expanded viewpoint in her comments on Bitcoin in these pages, framing it both in the context of precursor innovations in digital currency and in the framework of long-range planetary cycles and her astrological projections about the economic and financial trends likely to emerge in the coming decades.

Wendy Stacey, who like Christeen Skinner is from the United Kingdom, provides a sweeping overview and commentary on Bitcoin's emerging role. She details many of the current controversies and points of consternation about Bitcoin. She then offers a detailed analysis of the horoscope for the birth of Bitcoin with the creation of the Genesis Block in the distributed ledger that validates transactions, using it to forecast upcoming trends.

Gonçalo Moreira, from Barcelona, Spain, while relatively new to the study of astrology, adds his profound expertise in technical analysis of market dynamics to our understanding of Bitcoin's potential.

His observations on wave analysis and his skill in point-and-figure charting make his contribution to this book particularly valuable. Like the art of horoscope delineation, technical analysis of the markets is also a process of pattern recognition, so even though some of the analytical trading charts that Gonçalo presents in this book may not be familiar to some astrologers, they certainly have much to gain from the insights he presents and their implications for understanding cycle dynamics.

Bill Meridian's name has long been synonymous with expertise and integrity in astro-trading and mundane astrology. The unique insights that he shares with us from Vienna, Austria get right to the point in identifying a powerful transneptunian dynamic that he perceptively associates with the meteoric rise in the price of Bitcoin during the closing months of 2017.

My own contributions to this work are grounded in years of study and application of traditional astrological techniques, an in-depth exploration of Uranian and symmetrical astrology, and a continuing passion for empirical research into the correlations between planetary cycle dynamics and the movements of the markets. During the past three decades much of that ongoing investigation has been conducted through my role as editor at FinancialCyclesWeekly.com, the global leader in astro-trading education.

Aside from the challenges of trying to adhere to a rational course through the emotion-soaked landscape of Bitcoin lore and biased opinions, there have been several other unique considerations in putting together this volume.

First of all, there are unprecedented challenges to the methods and perspectives of conventional astrology when we consider events that take place in cyberspace. While the events that we are trying to understand take place at times that can be extraordinarily well-articulated, their location is paradoxically often quite hard to pin down.

Indeed, the essence of the internet itself, as well as the integrity of the blockchain that validates Bitcoin transactions, is inextricably embedded in simultaneity in multiple locations, or in no specific location at all. We propose a strategy and a set of guidelines for addressing this particular challenge in the section of this book in which we've compiled some of the horoscopes that we consider most relevant to the evolution of Bitcoin.

Secondly, Bitcoin trading is incredibly volatile and erratic,. Each new day in the life of Bitcoin brings us the possibility of astonishing fluctuations and gut-wrenching reversals. Any attempt to provide current price and trend information literally becomes hopelessly outdated within days, if not hours.

In editing this book we thus inevitably had to confront the problem of presenting accurate information while being faced with relentless time decay. But if we're going to engage in the antiquated but nevertheless intellectually satisfying and eminently useful practice of committing ink to sheets of paper bound together, that's a factor we just have to learn to live with.

Finally, our research into the history and development of Bitcoin never stops producing fresh and ever more intriguing details. Scandals, break-throughs, new regulations, and ICO announcements appear in the news al-most every day, adding a rich and ever-changing array of events demanding fresh analysis in our efforts to unravel the mysteries of Bitcoin.

And with Bitcoin now actively traded on markets around the world, we are compiling more and more reliable records of historical prices. The data persistently begs to be examined under the lens of astro-trading analysis. And to top things off, the successful development of Bitcoin has given birth to hundreds of other cryptocurrencies and blockchain applications as well.

In other words, this could have been a much, much bigger book. We have repeatedly been tempted to analyze more deeply, write more extensively, and add more and more pages to this volume. But we had to stop somewhere, just to get this book into print. It has thus been our choice to focus in these pages almost exclusively on Bitcoin and its potential, setting aside for now the desire to investigate other cryptocurrencies and blockchain spin-offs.

The net result is a book that is at once both out of date as soon as it is published and incomplete in its treatment of a vast and compelling subject. This obviously leaves the door open for a revised edition at a later date, or perhaps supplemental volumes with more observations on Bitcoin and the growing ranks of other alt-coins and cryptocurrencies.

For the time being, however, our wish is simply that you enjoy the observations we are sharing with you in these pages, and that you find at least a few ideas and insights that can help propel you toward success. If you have not already invested in Bitcoin or used it in transactions, perhaps you may also be encouraged to investigate it further and put a toe into the water.

At best, we hope that we have created a tool that you will turn to again and again for inspiration, for effective analytical and trading strategies, and for reliable resources to use in your own research and engagement with the markets.

And if you are an astrologer, a Bitcoin trader, or a market analyst, we also hope that you will be motivated to add your own observations and comments to future efforts in the quest to understand Bitcoin astrology. This is a field of investigation that is still very much in its infancy, and we need many creative and conscientious collaborators to help nurture and sustain it.

Tim Bost

May 2, 2018

Palmetto, Florida, USA

The Bitcoin Proposal Horoscope

Tim Bost

Astrology is all about the timing of events. When we cast a natal horoscope, the event is quite specific – the baby is born, the first rush of outside air enters the newborn lungs, and a cry of new life reverberates. But with mundane astrology and financial horoscopes, that birth process is often much less well-defined.

Two friends meet for drinks in an isolated corner of a local pub. The conversation turns to complaints about the status quo, and as the alcohol flows, oaths are sworn and loyalties pledged. Within a couple of weeks the gatherings at the pub have become regular events, and a dozen comrades are buying rounds and making boasts.

It isn't long before manifestos are written and pamphlets are secretly distributed. Within a few months weapons have been gathered, and the meetings at the pub have become secret sessions for strategic planning. The following year an armed revolt overthrows the old regime, and on a glorious Sunday morning a bright new flag flies over the capitol.

As astrologers, we of course note the time that flag was hoisted. We symbolically mark it as the moment of birth for the new nation. But when did that country – and the concept behind it – really begin? When the first shot was fired? When the first oath was sworn? When the first drink was poured?

The same kind of process is often evident in the development of a business. A conversation around the kitchen table leads to experimentation with new cookie recipes. The cookies are a big hit at the bake sale for the local scout troop, and it doesn't take too long for a new bakery to open its doors. The popularity of the baked goods soon leads to the establishment of a few more branches of the enterprise. Within a couple of years the now well-established brand takes its shares public.

We can date our financial horoscopes based on when the first bakery lease was signed, when the corporate papers were drawn up, or on when the shares were first traded on the stock exchange. But once again, the growth of an organized idea or enterprise is a gradual, somewhat amorphous process. It's rare that business begins with a single dramatic stroke accompanied by a thunderclap. Instead the start is typically a series of experiments, explorations, and somewhat tentative commitments. Little by little, they evolve into an entity that has its own life cycle of growth, vitality, and decline.

Precursor Horoscopes

The same kind of developmental arc also characterizes Bitcoin, with all of the usual uncertainties, rabbit trails, and opportunities for insight. While it is logical to look primarily to the Genesis Block recording of the first-ever

Bitcoin transaction as the birth event for the new cryptocurrency, there are also noteworthy precursor events which deserve our attention as well.

Richard Nixon's 1971 decision to end redemption of the U.S. Dollar for gold, allowing the currency to float relative to other currencies, is an important example. This action allowed for active trading and speculation in currency pairs, and was a pivotal move toward redefining the nature of currencies and the ultimate creation of cryptocurrencies as well.

The collapse of Lehman Brothers in September, 2008, a catastrophic event which triggered a global financial meltdown, was also a watershed event. As "the straw that broke the camel's back" in the financial markets, it was emblematic of a crisis that had been slowly developing behind the scenes for some time previously in an atmosphere of fiscal irresponsibility in high places. In many ways the ensuing near-collapse of international financial structures helped create the fertile soil that allowed the notion of an alternative payment system like Bitcoin to take root.

The posting of Satoshi Nakamoto's white paper defining the Bitcoin concept about two months prior to the Genesis Block was certainly a significant event. It laid the groundwork for the development of blockchain technologies which are already transforming life as we know it. But in that document there are references to the website bitcoin.org, with a domain name that had been registered in Panama several months prior to the online release of the Bitcoin proposal.

That registration event, with a much more well-articulated connection to the Bitcoin proposal itself, also helps provide a context for the understanding of Bitcoin and its ultimate implications for economic relationships. It is yet another precursor chart for us to consider.

We have provided all these charts, as well as other precursor horoscopes, in a later chapter in this book. They merit in-depth study by those who are seeking a richer, more comprehensive understanding of Bitcoin and its full implications.

The Proposal Horoscope

The horoscope for the Bitcoin proposal itself is especially noteworthy. It can be precisely timed because of its pedigree as a time-stamped posting on an internet discussion forum. And when we examine the planetary alignments which were in play at that specific time, we can see a symbolic portrait of Bitcoin and its remarkable long-term potential.

As is the case with many events associated with the development of Bitcoin, there are are a variety of recollections about exactly when the Satoshi Nakamoto white paper actually became public.

The date that appears on the document itself is October 31, 2008. But as far as we can tell, its actual release came with a forum post by Satoshi Nakamoto two days later. It apparently originated from a computer server in Singapore, which is where we've located this horoscope.

The proposal chart is noteworthy for a number of reasons. It is particularly remarkable because it shows such a tremendous potential for change.

The chart is set against the backdrop of a powerful Saturn/Uranus opposition. As the two outer planets meet in this alignment, they highlight potential struggles between traditional rules and conventional approaches on the one hand, and the forces of innovation and ingenuity on the other.

Saturn in Virgo is strongly focused on keeping score, pushing for precise measurements and the kind of responsible accounting that keeps established power structures in place. Uranus in intuitive Pisces explodes with unexpected opportunities for doing things in radical new ways. It is here to break the rules, not to keep them.

Bitcoin Proposal
Event Chart
Nov 2 2008, Sun
17:56:27 AWST -8:00
Singapore, Singapore
01°N17' 103°E51'
Geocentric
Tropical
Koch
True Node

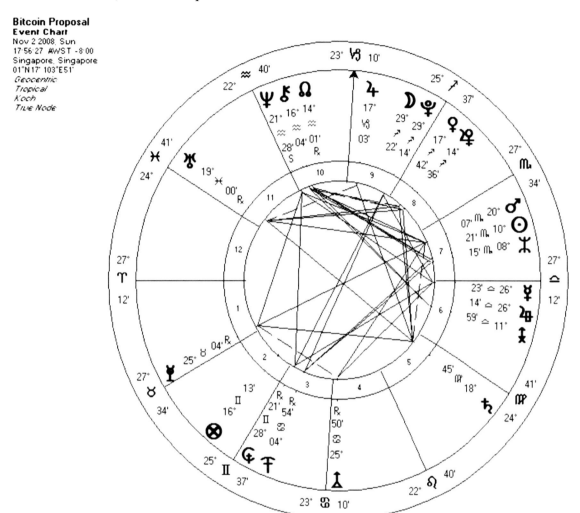

Mars, the ruler of the Ascendant and the dispositor of the Sun in this chart, plays an especially powerful role. In its essential dignity as the traditional ruler of Scorpio, it is ready to take intense and persistent action by converting the Saturn/Uranus standoff into an "easy opposition". It does so by adding a supportive trine to help anchor the emotional instability of Uranus, while at the same time forming a sextile to Saturn as a reminder that active analysis can open the door to the new and effective structures which may ultimately offer greater advantages than the old forms which are on the way out.

It's worth noting here as well that Saturn is receiving a calming and expansive trine from Jupiter. This suggests that even though this event takes place in tumultuous times, there is ample cause for optimism. Jupiter also does a lot to tone down the explosive energy of Uranus here, adding a magnanimous air of good-natured acceptance that can easily take the erratic behavior of Uranus in stride.

Remarkable Conjunctions

Two remarkable planetary conjunctions stand out sharply in this horoscope. They are noteworthy not only because of their tight orb, but also because of the speed of the planets involved, making them short-term occurrences which offer us specific opportunities for gaining deep insights into the intrinsic nature of this astrological event.

The first is the Moon/Pluto conjunction in the final degree of Sagittarius. In a mundane horoscope like this one, Pluto represents the potential for massive change, big expressions of power, and the movement of large amounts of money. The Moon, on the other hand, signifies the public at large, along with the actions and opinions of masses of people.

This tight conjunction thus signals the potential for more power to the people, the spreading of vast amounts of wealth to the masses, and the kinds of sweeping change that can totally reshape public consciousness. It is emblematic of the kind of peer-to-peer transactions and creative connections that can facilitate exactly that kind of transformation.

And, because of this conjunction's proximity to the cardinal axis World Point at 0° Capricorn, the "power to the people" promised here is not just for one nation or one particular constituency. It's for everyone on the planet.

The second strong conjunction, found at the Descendant in this horoscope, is the meeting of Mercury and the transneptunian factor Apollon. Mercury, of course, is a fast-moving planet of communications and information transfer, while Apollon indicates the expansion of commercial activity and the transmission of scientific and technical knowledge far and wide. Apollon brings a spatial dynamic to the mix, amplifying Mercury's ability to broadcast its message to diverse, far-flung locations.

The Mercury/Apollon conjunction is also an especially appropriate planetary representation of the role of the blockchain in creating a distributed network for verification of transactions. And for that matter, the powerful emphasis on Apollon in this chart also suggests the likelihood of a widespread replication of the blockchain technology introduced in the Bitcoin proposal, leading, as we have already seen, to a massive proliferation of other cryptocurrencies.

While this horoscope is rich in its implications for the potential positive impact of Bitcoin, it is not without some cautionary indicators as well. Note that the Moon/Pluto conjunction is in an opposition to the transneptunian factor Hades. This is a stark indicator of Bitcoin's potential contribution to the deterioration of moral standards, and to its intrinsic attractiveness for some rather unsavory characters, including individuals involved in criminal or anti-social activity.

While the Bitcoin proposal chart is not necessarily the most effective instrument for timing price movements in Bitcoin trading, it is nevertheless a striking horoscope that deserves careful examination and sustained reflection. The advent of Bitcoin is definitely not a trivial event, and this horoscope gives us many important clues about its ultimate significance in global affairs during the years ahead.

Outer Planet Cycles and
The Development of Bitcoin

Christeen Skinner

It is generally accepted that Bitcoin, the first decentralized cryptocurrency, was created in January 2009. The roots of this concept, however, can be traced back to 1983 when the American cryptographer David Chaum, working on an electronic money system, conceived of e-cash. We must assume that he had been incubating the idea for some time.

If we are to correlate this development with action within the solar system, we could begin by setting this development in global financial activity against the backdrop of the sunspot cycle. Solar Cycle 24 began in early 2008 – presumably as this new financial concept gained traction.

Although it seems that there is definite correlation between developments in cryptocurrencies and planetary cycles, solar activity may be no less important may. We'll discuss it in more detail later in this article.

From the purely planetary perspective, it is possible that the real roots of this new form of currency coincided with the Jupiter Saturn cycle and their conjunction in Libra in 1981.

Jupiter and Saturn align approximately every 20 years. There is a pattern to their conjunctions which take place in one element (fire, earth, air or water) over a 240-year period before crossing into the next element.

The important thing here is that the penultimate conjunction occurs in the new element. The conjunction of 1981 heralded the 240-year Air sequence that begins at the winter solstice in 2020 and is interrupted only by the penultimate of that series in 2999, which heralds the move to a quarter of a millennium of Jupiter-Saturn conjunctions in Fire signs.

The 1981 conjunction was in an Air sign. Air signs are all about ideas – not tangibles. It is perhaps unremarkable that during the 1981 Air cycle, that many of the now classified "weapons of mass financial destruction" were developed between 1981 and 2000 (the last conjunction of the Earth series).

In 2020, the next Air conjunction occurs. The genie, genius of ideas-based currencies, is unlikely to fit back into the bottle.

Before exploring this further, consider: in 2020, and only a few months ahead of the coming Jupiter-Saturn conjunction in Aquarius, an extraordinary alignment of planets takes place. This last occurred at the end of the 13th Century. It is interesting, in the light of recent questioning of the true value of cryptocurrencies, that Thomas Aquinas, a great sage of the 13th Century, stressed the importance of "an unchanging coin and recognition of the true value of things".

He was surely correct in identifying the financial risks being taken by rulers of that time. The credit crisis of 1294 was monumental. Philip IV of

France refused to honour his debts. His subsequent behaviour then set off a cascade of banking failure.

My view is that any forecast of how cryptocurrencies might operate in the coming years has to be viewed against the background of probable banking re-alignment (at best) or of total collapse (at worst) between 2020 and another singular cosmic alignment in 2026.

The "new" currency of the 13th Century was the Florin (the coin of Florence, Italy). Its birth did not lead to the subsequent banking collapse – that was due to default on debt. Yet the parallels between the 13th Century and the present time though are simple: arrival of new currency, banking development and then mis – or - dishonourable behaviour.

History does not have to repeat, but any overview of the new cryptocurrencies should take into account the probable developments essential in the banking industry to cope with these new financial instruments, including risk assessment of probable default on loans that use these cryptocurrencies.

Jupiter and Saturn reached the Full Moon phase (when they opposed one another) of their 1981 Libra conjunction on five occasions (from a geo-centric perspective and therefore incorporating retrograde positions). These oppositions took place between 1989 and 1991, by which time Saturn had moved into Aquarius (where it will also be after December 20th 2020).

In 1990, and against the background of the Jupiter-Saturn opposition, David Chaum, originator of e-cash, founded a new company, DigiCash. This company filed for bankruptcy soon after the two planets came to the last quarter phase of their cycle.

The concept of electronic cash had by now captured the imagination of many – no doubt spurred by the arrival of Neptune (ethereal) in future-ideas-oriented Aquarius in 1998; it was marked by the emergence of Pay-Pal and of E-gold during that same decade.

Whilst the paper-work describing the nature and operating system for Bitcoin was available in late 2008, arguably the most significant chart for this new currency is a recognized transaction made in Sydney, Australia on January 3rd, 2009 – though we have seen other charts: including one for January 4th at 03:45 in Tokyo, Japan.

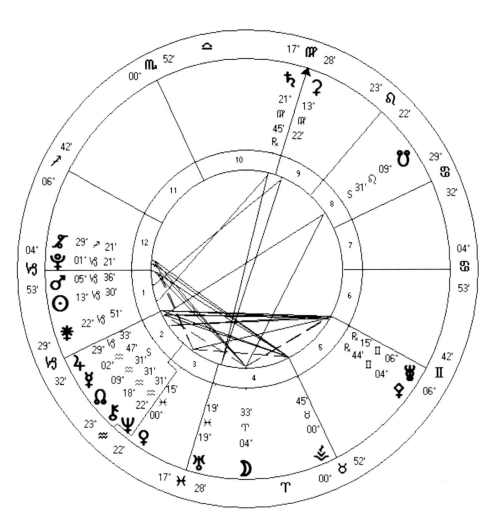

Bitcoin Australia
Natal Chart
Jan 3 2009, Sat
18:15:05 GMT +0:00
Sydney, AU
33°S52' 151°E13'
Geocentric
Tropical
Koch
True Node

Cracking Bitcoin's Astro-Code

Whichever chart is used, the fact is that Bitcoin came to greater public consciousness as Saturn and Uranus came to their opposition.

It is important to understand the nature of this hugely important planetary cycle. The Jupiter-Saturn cycle has clear links with a recognized twenty year business cycle. By contrast, the Saturn-Uranus cycle is all about challenge to the status quo. These two planets opposed one another toward the end of World War 1, when I think that most people would accept that societies changed forever. They did so again in 1965 – another period of extraordinary social upheaval. Saturn and Uranus opposed one another most recently at the global financial crisis of 2008.

There is little doubt that following on from the global financial crisis, many no longer had respect for the banking system or for the governments that sought to control it. The time was ripe for a new system to emerge.

It is interesting that Bitcoin is built on a block (Saturn) chain (Uranus) technology. Coming into being at the Saturn-Uranus opposition or Full Moon phase, we can be reasonably sure that by the time the two planets reach their next conjunction (in 2031), that this system will be regarded as the status quo.

Clearly crucial to Bitcoin's success is its usability. Until such time as Bitcoin could be traded easily for gold or some other product or service, its true "currency" is limited.

Bitcoin initially blossomed on the so-termed "Dark Web" where it posed – and continues to pose - headaches for governments, in that one of its great attractions (anonymity) meant that it could be used for all types of shady dealings or money laundering. With little traceability, tax could not be collected. Bitcoin then - and now - is a serious challenge to governments across the world.

In any of the charts for January 2009, the Sun and asteroid Ceres are in trine to one another at 13° of, respectively, Capricorn and Virgo. The ease with which Bitcoin has operated within the dark web is indicated by this aspect.

The proliferation of Bitcoin trades - both legitimate and in secret and dark transactions - is probable throughout 2018 as Neptune opposes Ceres whilst simultaneously sextiling the Sun. Indeed, it may be that governments themselves make use of this currency – whilst also, perhaps, inaugurating their own versions of blockchain money.

There is another vital placement in those early January 2009, Bitcoin charts: the asteroid Vesta's position at 0° Taurus. Vesta may be thought of as the trader's asteroid. In the charts of traders I have worked with, this asteroid is usually prominently placed.

In this chart Vesta is at right-angle to Mercury (planet of commercial dealing), again affirming that Bitcoin came into being at the 'right cosmic time'.

In May 2018, Uranus enters Taurus for the first time since 1934. This in itself will surely bring political, social and economic disruption. It will surely also see marked fluctuation in Bitcoin's price. Bearing in mind that as Uranus moves into Taurus, Mars simultaneously moves into Aquarius where it aligns with Bitcoin's "natal" Mercury, it is reasonable to anticipate days of high volatility that month.

In March 2017, Bitcoin was given a price against gold. This marked a considerable development. The event occurred just a few weeks ahead of Saturn's 120° relationship to Uranus (exact on May 19th 2017) and is in keeping with Bitcoin's increasing presence and recognition on the global financial stage.

We should expect further developments throughout 2019 and 2020 as Saturn and Uranus form a bi-septile aspect to one another. What might this mean? In all probability these curious aspects will coincide with Bitcoin's increased use on both the Dark Web and in International Arts trading.

There are many other fascinating features to the early January charts: the grouping (or stellium) of Mercury, Vertex, North Node, Chiron, Neptune and Venus in airy Aquarius drawing immediate attention. We should note too that Jupiter was in the very last degree of Capricorn. Using solar arc progressions, Jupiter crossed into Aquarius within Bitcoin's first year of trading: arguably giving it a rocket-boost launch.

That same technique points to Venus' move into Pisces within the first year of trading. This does not augur quite so well: suggesting confused and fluctuating value that would be unlikely to settle until after solar arc Moon moved into Aries in the second year of trading.

At the declination level, Mars was out of bounds at Bitcoin's launch (another indicator of potential volatility) whilst Saturn and Vesta are in parallel and both at contra-parallel to Uranus. This is a highly unusual configuration suggesting potential longevity but also inherent instability.

At the time of writing, there are over 1400 crypto or blockchain currencies in existence: many of which have come into being since August 2011, when Neptune moved into Pisces. (It's interesting that Google Wallet was introduced just a month later). The concept of digital, e-cash, or cryptocurrencies is not going to go away; though lack of regulation is of great concern.

Attempts have been made to define virtual currencies, though in keeping with attempts to do this as Neptune moves through Pisces, there is as yet no agreed terminology. Even so, it is recognized that the conditions are ripe for digital currencies in that they can reduce operating costs, increase efficiency and enable a wide range of new applications. Central banks are engaged in wide discussion to include a central bank issued digital currency.

Astrologers might agree that this course of action is already set among the stars and will be in operation within months of the Jupiter-Saturn conjunction in late 2020.

The Future For Bitcoin

In December 2017, Bitcoin's price soared to over $16,000. Its price has since crashed spectacularly as Saturn moved from Sagittarius to Capricorn.

Since Bitcoin's first trade in 2009, Saturn has changed signs on three occasions: from natal Virgo, to Libra, then to Scorpio, then Sagittarius and most recently to Capricorn. These earlier ingresses did not have singular effect on the price. That situation changed as Saturn moved into Capricorn at the Winter Solstice 2017. The peak was actually a few days ahead of this – and coincided with the Progressed Moon (Australia chart), exactly opposed the natal Mars position.

Bitcoin reached a low ($5,962) on February 6th: almost exactly halfway between the lunar eclipse of January 31st 2018 and the accompanying solar eclipse on February 15th, 2018. The lunar eclipse was itself at right angles to the lunar nodal position in the natal chart as Saturn, by transit, squared natal Mars (coming up against a brick wall).

The Saturn transit repeats a few days ahead of the next solar eclipse (July 12th, 2018) and again in early November 2018 as Jupiter moves from Scorpio to Sagittarius and so squares natal Venus. Both periods should be viewed as delicate or volatile with probable dramatic moves.

A striking feature of the natal chart is the positioning of Jupiter, Venus and the Moon each at the end of signs and Venus at the midpoint of Moon/Jupiter. From this we can deduce that Bitcoin has star-attraction and secondly that ANY planet's ingress will coincide with a ripple in the share price. The extent of that ripple will vary according to the nature of the planet and sign involved.

As we saw, the only Saturn ingress so far to coincide with profound effect was its Capricorn ingress. Similarly, it was Jupiter's recent Scorpio ingress that can be shown to have acted as rocket fuel to the price. Earlier ingresses did not have as dramatic an effect. I suspect that it would be wrong to discount the effect of slower-moving planet ingresses as yet: Bitcoin is, after all, still a "teenager" in terms of its age.

A more valuable exercise is review of Mars' ingresses. Mars has now completed a circuit of the Bitcoin chart five times. We then have a reasonable number - 60 ingresses - to review. A ripple effect is apparent as the planet moves from one sign to another. It is worth noting that Bitcoin's price tends to fall as the planet moves through one of the Fixed signs i.e. XBTUSD is lower as Mars moves into the next Mutable sign after its move into a Fixed sign.

Cryptos And The Sun

Bitcoin has now been around for almost an entire sunspot cycle (approximately 11.2 years). That so many other cryptos have emerged as the sunspot activity reached its peak, is perhaps unsurprising. Of these, two have emerged as potential claimants for the crypto throne: Ethereum and Ripple. Even if Bitcoin were to "die" one or other of those – or another entirely – would surely continue.

Cryptos may well be an idea or concept whose time has come. Those cryptos yet to launch – and especially those launching in December 2020 as the sunspot cycle reaches minimum and that extraordinary planetary alignment takes place, may be the ones to watch. Investments in these could pay off by the next Saturn-Uranus conjunction in 2031.

Perhaps though the best investment of all, would be in crypto mining and in those individuals with the necessary expertise in this rapidly advancing field.

Copyright © Christeen Skinner, 11 March 2018

Bitcoin – A Gateway For Which There Is No Return!

Wendy Stacey

Cryptocurrencies are digital or virtual currencies which are controlled by the masses. There are no regulations to adhere to, and they provide a free and open source model in which people can invest, trade and potentially make use of them as a form of purchasing power. Being decentralized, they cut out the banks and financial regulators.

In its embryonic form, the concept of cryptocurrencies initially attracted a younger generation for "get rich quick" schemes, as well as the financial and tech geeks who could actually understand the concept. Not surprisingly it appealed to a generation whose lives had been disadvantaged by rising education fees, by whopping student loans, by competition to get a desired job, and by persistent doubts about ever getting onto the property ladder.

This new industry provides at the very least a new way of looking at how the world could operate. As awareness of the cryptocurrency industry has grown, so have the opportunities, and the several digitally-based currencies now on offer have caught the attention of everyone around the globe. What cryptocurrencies have enabled (with Pluto through Capricorn) is the creation of power to the collective and a means of getting rid of the corrupt, dogmatic and unworkable regulations and the unnecessary middlemen within the financial industries. Whether Bitcoin or other cryptocurrencies continue in their current format remains to be seen, but what they have already achieved is a new monetary system from which there is no return.

Bitcoin was the first cryptocurrency to be formed. It was created by an anonymous person named Satoshi Nakamoto and the Ledger start date began on 04 January 2009, Tokyo, Japan at 3:15 a.m[i].

As Pluto had ingressed into Capricorn we witnessed the collapse of our banking and financial industries. Despite the negative reputation of cryptocurrencies, it is arguable that this new runaway financial market has been born out of the lack of confidence in both the regulation and security offered by our existing financial markets and governments. Change and innovation are inevitably born out of volatility and insecurity.

It is important to note that there is no value to a Bitcoin (it is merely a private key) but in the same way, there is no value of the paper for a 50-dollar bill. The bill holds a higher value than its paper due to its encrypted printing.

The same can be said for Bitcoin in terms of its encrypted algorithm. They are similar in that they are both a medium of exchange within a monetary system, and are both vulnerable to losing or increasing their global exchange value.

China leads in Bitcoin mining and it is thought that the nation's mining holds over 70% of the world's mining pools[ii]. The Chinese government is intent on driving miners of cryptocurrencies out of the country [due to concerns about electricity usage] and there is talk of moving a significant amount of the country's mining operation to Canada.[iii]

Iceland is expected to double its energy consumption due to the mining of cryptocurrencies.[iv] The global environmental impact due to mining is a growing argument against the digital monetary system. It is estimated that each Bitcoin transaction will use 275 kWh of electricity.[v] So, we might find in the near future mining pools being limited (or relocated) due to increasing prices of electricity or to the restricting of its usage.

This is a controversial issue, as mining companies around the world are arguing that the energy consumption used in internet surfing and research, as well as for credit card transactions, also consume energy, and that the global impact of Bitcoin mining is no different.

Financial regulators are also apprehensive that people are borrowing money to purchase Bitcoin, which is increasing the level of personal debt. Due to current decentralization and the inability to regulate (therefore making it difficult to tax, assess risk, or control the market), cryptocurrencies are continuously attacked by existing financial institutions, their leaders and key players as they propose a threat to the existing structures of how we purchase, transact, invest and build assets.

There is also the argument for the potential to launder money. As a controversial investment, Jamie Dimon, boss of JPMorgan Chase, has called the cryptocurrency industry a "fraud". Economist Nourriel Roubini has labeled it a "gigantic speculative bubble".

As with anything on the internet there is a vulnerability for hacking. Recent heists include the December 2017 hijack where hackers targeted South Korea's Bithumb exchange, stealing over $7 million in digital money and the personal information of 30,000 people. The hackers then demanded another $5.5 million to delete the traders' personal information.[vi]

In early 2018, a server which hosts wallets (the digital device that stores people's currencies controlled by a private key), was hijacked and $400,000 was transferred to an untraceable alternative virtual currency.[vii] In March 2018 what is now named the "Big Bitcoin Heist", saw 11 people arrested in Iceland for stealing 600 cryptocurrency mining servers from data centres across the country.[viii]

There is worry that quantum computers might pose a threat to Bitcoin and other virtual currencies, although it might be that cryptocurrencies adopt and invest in quantum computers to keep ahead of the game.

Whilst some countries are banning using cryptocurrencies (such as China), others are embracing it. In January 2018 Economy Minister to Switzerland, Johann Schneider-Ammann stated "The country [Switzerland] should seek to become the 'crypto-nation'".[ix] The village of Zug aims to be the capital [crypto-valley] of that nation. The village has a corporation tax rate of 8.5% and has become an attractive hub for crypto firms.

We may find mining hubs increasing around the world where data centres, cryptocurrency companies and potentially consumers might migrate to. We could expect mini-cities being erected which resemble Gibraltar or Monte Carlo, although probably located in areas of Asia where electricity is abundant and where there is a larger labour force for technological progression. The existence of locations where cryptocurrencies are not welcomed may give rise to black markets around the globe.

This global controversy extends to students of Ivy League schools demanding that teaching on cryptocurrencies and the blockchain be implemented into their MBA programmes. Harvard and Stanford will be introducing this instruction in 2018 and already Stanford's programme is oversubscribed.[x] We can expect from this trend the emergence of a highly educated generation which will work and develop this model, from which there is no going back.

Below is the chart for Bitcoin. The first thing one would notice in this radix chart is the heavy Saturnian qualities about it. It has a strong stellium in Capricorn in the second house, along with Jupiter at a potent 29°. This bodes well for a financial market, giving it a strong backbone, a sound base, and a paternal quality. Those who drive the market activity in Bitcoin will be relentless, hardworking and ambitious.

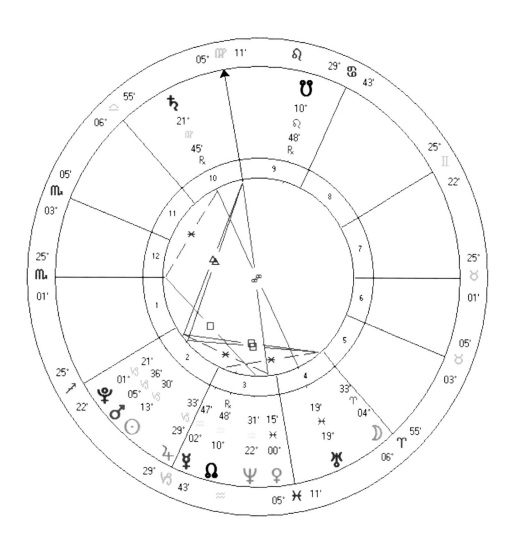

Bitcoin
Natal Chart
Jan 4 2009 Sun
03:15 JST -9:00
Tokyo, Japan
35°N42' 139°E46'
Geocentric
Tropical
Placidus
Mean Node

These four planets in Capricorn are ruled by Saturn in Virgo in the tenth house, the most elevated planet in the chart, sitting as the handle of the bucket shape, reinforcing the fences it erects. Posited in Virgo, it perhaps describes the puzzle-solving and checking others' proof of work within the mining, as well as the ledger that records, files and stores all the transactions. It is not surprising with such a heavy Saturnian chart that the key argument against Bitcoin's very existence is "regulation". This is the monetary system's greatest weakness, but also its strength. The Saturnian quality also denotes the limited nature of the supply that Bitcoin can generate.

Saturn in the chart is separating from an opposition with Uranus, which might depict a trend in the economy that is about releasing the shackles of financial and economic oppression by heavy regulation and conformity (which proved not to work), along with quantitative easing that produces further debt and thus the pursuit of an open source and free movement where people have control over their own resources (to a certain extent). With all its emphasis on Saturn and Capricorn, along with a Scorpio Ascendant, the chart seems reasonably bulletproof and appears to have a good sound business base.

A Scorpio Ascendant also provides for anonymity. Mercury in Aquarius (the ruler of the MC) resides in the third house and is ideal for a highly intellectual (to the point of people being unable to understand its process), data-generating, high-tech innovation which has spearheaded new communities and forms of interaction and calculation unprecedented in human history.

As Mercury is separating from a conjunction to Jupiter, these two planets combined will do a great job selling the "belief" that the sky is the limit or you just can't lose. This pioneering, brave, high-energy but continuously challenging initiative is also echoed by an Aries Moon which is building to a square to Mars. Venus at another powerful degree sits at 0° of Pisces in the third house describing the universal spread of attraction, the illusion and seductive power of a get-rich-quick scheme. As Venus is separating from a conjunction to Neptune, this repeats the illusion theme, and as inflation is often associated with the planet Neptune, then the desire to invest and have faith in the dream, is not only rather desirable, but also actually possible.

Bitcoin has had some dips recently and below is the price index for Bitcoin from mid-2017 to early March 2018. November and early-mid December 2017 saw two large dips and a large one on the 30th of December.

Chart courtesy of Bitcoin.com

What seems to be clear is that the chart of Bitcoin is certainly sensitive to Saturn transits, which is not surprising given that Bitcoin has four planets in Capricorn (Pluto, Mars, Sun and Jupiter) which reside in the second house. Bitcoin had a huge dip in its price index when transiting Saturn conjoined the radix Pluto at 1° of Capricorn (within 11 minutes of arc). Uranus was slowing down, remained and stationed at 24° 34' of Aries between 28 December 2017 until 07 January 2018.

The largest dip for Bitcoin was on 6 February 2018 when transiting Saturn conjoined Bitcoin's radix Mars at 5° of Capricorn (within 16 minutes of arc). Mars is Bitcoin's co-chart ruler. In addition to this, the total lunar eclipse (involving the super blue blood Moon) on the 31st January 2018 conjoined the chart of Bitcoin's nodes (within 49 minutes of arc).

The following are dates where the Bitcoin chart is triggered by transits. They are speculative and should be considered as such but are provided so the radix chart can be tracked over the next three years. Of course, it is always easier for astrologers to see the bear and bull periods in markets in hindsight, but observing the chart of Bitcoin can help us understand the sensitive areas in the chart.

Future Challenging Dates

17 March 2018

At the time of writing (early March) this transit has not yet come to occur. Transiting Mars will leave the gambling and inflated sign of Sagittarius and enter Capricorn which will have a temporary squeeze on trade.

15 May 2018

Transiting Uranus enters Taurus which may create a slump for all financial markets. This could indicate a slowing down temporarily, but could also create an interesting technological surge in moving forward after some time. Perhaps we will see new innovations in Bitcoin's usage, in its purchasing power, and in the enhancement of mining in some form.

1 July 2018

Transiting Saturn in its retrograde journey will travel back over Bitcoin's radix Mars. This could certainly slow things down for Bitcoin. Mars is the co-ruler for Bitcoin and Saturn here puts the brakes on. This could be in relation to slowing down transactions, or it could connect with issues having to do with regulation. Either way, it would normally indicate stopping any progression during this time. Saturn will go retrograde again in August and make its last conjunction when it is direct on 09 November 2018.

11 August 2018

The solar partial eclipse will highlight 18° of Leo/Aquarius which conjoins Bitcoin's radix Chiron. Transiting Uranus in Taurus will square the radix Mercury (within 14 minutes of arc) and transiting retrograde Mars will be on its way back to conjoin the radix Jupiter (it will be exact on 15 August). This period may not fare well for Bitcoin during this period (considering the January eclipse and when transiting Saturn conjoined Pluto and Mars on the first conjunction in Capricorn). The hits to Mercury and the third house might indicate some media hype (particularly on the potential of quantum or super computers) or further hacking. Mining communities and mini hubs may be targeted during this time. Alterative sources may begin offering ways of copying the crypto-virtual model, but adapting a currency to it in a more regulated way. Halting the transaction process, perhaps with credit card or banking facilities may also be an issue that gets raised during this time.

19 January 2019

Transiting Saturn conjoins Bitcoin's radix Sun. This will challenge the very heart and identity (name and perhaps founder) of the company. Saturn does come back in October 2019 and comes within a degree of conjoining the radix Sun again but does not make an exact conjunction.

11 May 2019

Transiting Chiron will conjoin Bitcoin's Moon at 04° 32' of Aries (there is however a grand sextile of Jupiter in Sagittarius, albeit retrograde, and Venus at 25° 09' in Aries to Bitcoin's Neptune at 22° 31 of Aquarius on the same day). Transiting Mars is also separating from a trine to this Neptune. The Moon in Aries represents the pioneering aspect of this chart so the competition or perhaps even the founder might come under unwanted spotlight. As the people are represented by the Moon in the chart and as Chiron is triggering it, then it doesn't fare well for those involved in it.

3 December 2019

Transiting Jupiter will exit Sagittarius and enter Capricorn. When a planet resides in Sagittarius it exaggerates gambling, hope, speculation and optimism. Once it leaves this sign and ingresses into Capricorn, the rules and regulations needed to rectify what went out of control in the previous sign, are implemented.

12 January 2020

The Saturn-Pluto conjunction at 22° Capricorn will undoubtedly shake up the financial institutions and markets during this period. This is indicative of enforcing regulatory practices, introducing new policies on governance and policing which will not favour cryptocurrencies. This conjunction will be about the desperate need to enforce! However, this conjunction also spotlights the corruption within regulatory practice and policy so may bring a double-edged sword to the conflict. That the conjunction is trine to Bitcoin's Saturn might help delay a shake up for Bitcoin, however whilst transiting Uranus remains square to Bitcoin's Mercury (but trine to Bitcoin's Pluto) it may be forced to introduce new practices or adopt those from new cryptocurrencies which have implemented regulation into their model.

16 March - 3 April 2020

Transiting Neptune is building to a conjunction at 19° with Bitcoin's radix Uranus (which opposes the radix Saturn) whilst transiting Saturn conjoins Bitcoin's radix Jupiter. This period is interesting as the first transit could be quite positive, extending the reach of the technology and inflating the currency, however, at the same time, Saturn puts a squeeze on Jupiter (the chart's second house ruler) so taking it up the price index is unlikely.

21 June 2020

The solar annular eclipse at 00° 21' Cancer will oppose Bitcoin's Jupiter (within 48 minutes of arc) which again, will bring Bitcoin under an unwanted spotlight. An opposition usually involves an "other" and at a powerful degree like this one, it could be expected that new conflict may arise – perhaps through competition or circumstances involving legal issues.

Future Positive Dates

30 July 2018

Transiting Jupiter will sextile Bitcoin's Sun whilst transiting Mars will be separating from a conjunction to Bitcoin's radix Mercury (whilst transiting Venus will conjoin Bitcoin's Saturn). This looks to be a very positive period for Bitcoin. It is quite possible that more financial suppliers (for example, credit card companies) will offer to accept Bitcoin. The reputation of Bitcoin during this period looks favourable.

16 October 2018

Transiting Jupiter will conjoin Bitcoin's radix Ascendant at 25° 01' Scorpio, which will bring wanted attention. Jupiter on the Ascendant is about expansion and extension which could bring positive results for Bitcoin.

9 November 2018

Transiting Jupiter enters Sagittarius. Jupiter is comfortable in its own sign of speculation here.

21 December 2020

It is important to note that when Jupiter and Saturn conjoin in Aquarius at 0° (the start of an uninterrupted sequence of conjunctions of Jupiter and Saturn in the Air element since 1226, which will last until the year 2219), the world as we know it will change dramatically and virtual currencies will become mainstream markets of the economy. How this will be done is beyond our social imagination at present but Bitcoin gives us a glimpse of what is to come. As we enter this 'Air' period, we will experience an unprecedented era of super high technology (that will no longer be based on bricks and mortar)[xi] and where information and knowledge, speed and international access will be primary[xii].

Bitcoin may not last indefinitely (its Saturn opposition and return will be the true test) but will certainly be the paternal prototype to which other models will follow.

It has already been born, it can only improve, and there is certainly no turning back!

Endnotes

i Thank you to Maurice Fernandez, Geoff Gronlund and contributors (Patra, Nadya, Angela) for the charts and discussion on the OPA forum – they have an excellent webinar recorded I recommend those interested in this subject to join up and watch it.

ii Buy Bitcoin Worldwide: https://www.buyBitcoinworldwide.com/mining/china/ [accessed 01 March 2018]

iii CNN News: http://money.cnn.com/2018/02/09/technology/Bitcoin-mining-china-canada/index.html [accessed 09 February 2018]

iv CBC News: http://www.cbc.ca/news/technology/Bitcoin-energy-iceland-1.4532930 [accessed 13 February 2018]

v The London Economic https://www.thelondoneconomic.com/news/currency-burns-energy-Bitcoin-uses-electricity-159-countries/03/12/ [accessed 01 March 2018]

vi BBC News http://www.bbc.co.uk/news/world-asia-42378638 [17 December 2017]

vii BBC News http://www.bbc.co.uk/news/technology-42689642 [accessed 16 January 2018]

viii ITPRO: http://www.itpro.co.uk/strategy/28261/Bitcoin-news [accessed 05 March 2018]

ix The Economist: https://www.economist.com/news/finance-and-economics/21737255-switzerland-embraces-digital-currencies-and-crypto-entrepreneurs-banking-centre [accessed 06 March 2018]

x The Economist: https://www.economist.com/whichmba/cryptocurrencies-and-business-schools-risking-it-all-Bitcoin [accessed 04 March 2018]

xi Those currencies associated with names such as 'Litecoin' or that possess 'air' names (as we have seen with Airbnb) and whose charts resonate more with air than with earth (or other elements) will probably do better than the gateway founder Bitcoin.

Xii W. Stacey, 2017, "The 2020 Jupiter-Saturn Mutation Conjunction in Air", *The Astrological Journal*, July/August 2017

Bitcoin, Technically Speaking

Gonçalo Moreira

While astrology offers us many valuable insights into the nature of the financial markets and the potentially profitable trading opportunities the markets represent, the real power of astro-trading is most evident when astrology isn't used in isolation, but when it is combined with other tools for market analysis.

In my own experience, I've found that Technical Analysis, the study and assessment of historic and current trading charts, is one of the most reliable ways of visualizing and understanding the real potential of the markets.

Charting Scales, A Matter Of Time Horizon

In order to start approaching Bitcoin with Technical Analysis let's look at two different ways to chart its price history. The most commonly used method is through Arithmetic scaling as seen on the following page.

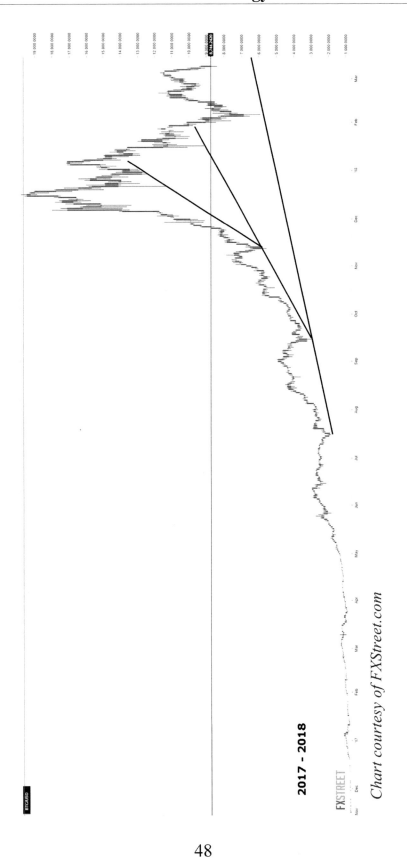

Chart courtesy of FXStreet.com

Arithmetic charts show the price units along the vertical scan line at equal price intervals. On an Arithmetic scale, low volatile price action does not look as active as high volatile price action.

Because of the high volatility displayed in Bitcoin's price, traders looking to capture short-term price movements or wanting to analyze trading ranges may prefer Arithmetic scales for price purity.

Alternatively, on a Ratio or Semi-Logarithmic scale, the vertical distance on the chart represents the same percentage change in price, instead of simply showing the numeric increments in price movement. This emphasis on ratios and percentages means that a 100% advance from 100 to 200 looks the same on the chart as a 100% advance from 10,000 to 20,000, even though the first advance is one hundred dollars and the second advance is ten thousand dollars.

Investors interested in following trends will likely prefer Ratio scaling. The rule of thumb for when a trader or analyst should be using an Arithmetic scale or a Ratio scale is that when the security's price range over the period being investigated is in the several-digit percentages, a Ratio scale is more accurate and thus typically more useful.

As you can see comparing both charts, long-term support and resistance lines are much easier to plot on a Ratio scale than on an Arithmetic scale, where the lines are steeper and easier to be cleared by price action.

In the Ratio scale chart shown on the following page, the steeper one of the three lines provided the beleaguered Bitcoin with support following the correction which started in December 2017. Bitcoin did not survive a second assault by shorts and its price slid below this line, to meet support upon the second lowest ascending line.

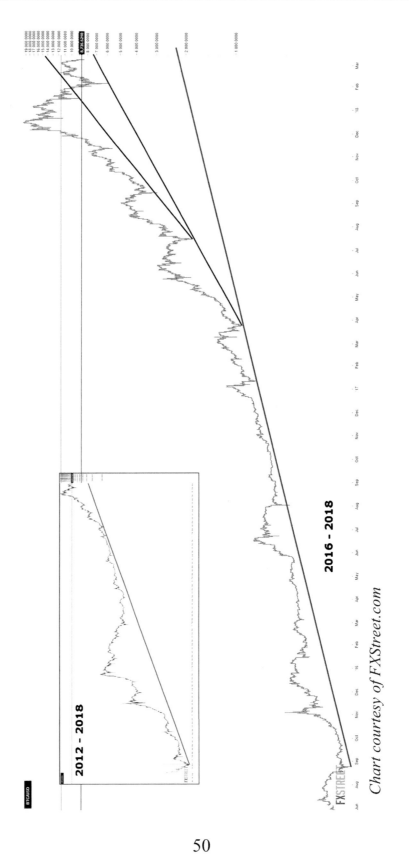

Chart courtesy of FXStreet.com

Notice how the first line changed polarity to resistance and capped the buying pressure from February 2018. Currently looming between 2,000 and 3,000 we find a third major support (red line), which should act as a hindrance – and as a price target for short sellers – if the second line is broken.

Another advantage of the Ratio scale consists in a better displaying of the speed of advances in the price of Bitcoin. On an Arithmetic scale, the price structure before 2017 (under 2,000 USD per Bitcoin) appears as a flat line, hiding important clues as to the speed of advance Bitcoin was able to show in its early years. It also shows that vibrant periods such as the one during 2017 were actually not uncommon in the past.

When we observe these periods on a chart with a Ratio scale, we can see that Bitcoin appears to go through periods of relative stability and then enter a phase of parabolic growth, followed by a sharp correction. Until now, all these corrections ended at higher levels than the pre-hype price, after which the greed phase of the cycle eventually begins again.

Momentum – The Quality Of A Trend

Investors need to be able to anticipate changes in price behavior so they can join a trend in its early stages, and also so they can get out of the market as soon as its trend stops being operative.

Momentum indicators are best suited for this type of endeavor since they measure the speed, i.e. the price trend's changing slope, and subsequently the acceleration and deceleration in price.

Speed is a more sensitive measurement than price itself, and acceleration is more sensitive than speed. For this reason, Momentum indicators are considered leading indicators of price change.

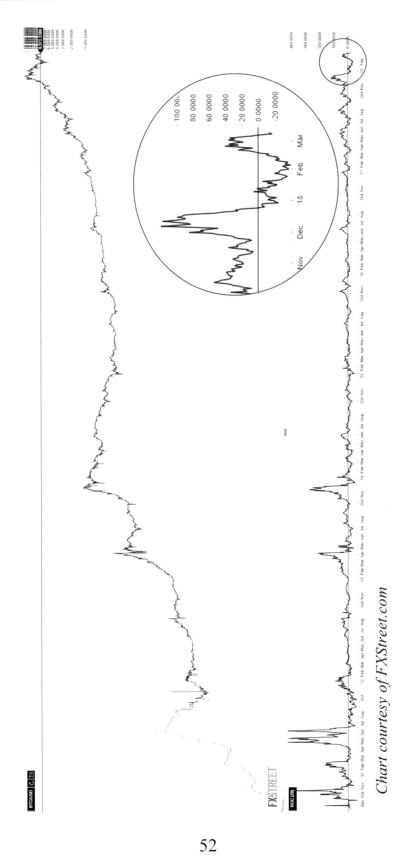

Chart courtesy of FXStreet.com

For example: if the 5-day rate of change in price is an increase of 100, then Momentum is 100, while the speed is 20 (100/5 = 20). When prices climb higher at a constant rate, Momentum indicators turn sideways. They only start declining when prices continue to climb but at a lower rate.

Therefore, declining Momentum does not necessarily mean that prices are falling, but it can be an early signal that prices may start correcting in the near future.

The nature of a Momentum indicator can be best understood when looking at a chart such as the one on the preceding page, covering Bitcoin's price history since 2013. Notice how the 2017 parabolic advance, once it is measured in terms of Rate of Change – Momentum in it purest form – has been abnormal, but it has certainly not been unprecedented.

The fact that recent Bitcoin advances have been less sharp in terms of Momentum than earlier ones has to be seen in relationship with nominal price advances. These moves would have to be truly spectacular in price terms in order to bring the Momentum indicator to a new high. That's because Momentum indicators need acceleration in prices, that is, more dollars recovered per period of time, in order to manifest a rising line.

It seems widely agreed this new class of Crypto assets manifested a bubble phase. But bubbles have a nasty way of expanding to a far larger level than generally expected.

Using an 20-month Rate Of Change (ROC) as a benchmark, we can see that previous "bubble phases" actually peaked at higher Momentum levels than the recent 2017 rally.

From a Momentum perspective, Bitcoin hasn't exhibited a true bubble as of late, but it definitely has the potential to do so.

Viewing market action from the perspective of Momentum has a great deal to offer. In fact, there are all sorts of signals for entering and exiting trades based on Momentum, but which fall out of scope of the current study.

We invite you to explore divergences between new highs and lows in price versus the indicator, to plot trend lines on the indicator itself to get breakout signals, and to watch zero-line crossovers in the Momentum line. These are perhaps the most common applications you can use to fine-tune both your long and short commitments in Bitcoin.

Elliott Wave - Prepared To Meander

A characteristic of the Elliott Wave Principle is that it allows us to analyze a market by starting either with a higher time frame chart and subsequently moving to lower time frames (top-down analysis), or by starting with a short-term one and moving then to higher time frames (down-top analysis).

Wave patterns can form in any time frame. This inherently fractal nature of the Elliott Wave Principle gives us an immense number of clues about the position of the market within its current price structure, and allows us to analyze it from any angle. Keep in mind that the goal when using Elliott Wave analysis is not to come up with the perfect wave count, but to determine the best probability scenario.

Bitcoin started a so-called "corrective pattern" from the all-time high close to 20,000 USD per Bitcoin with an A-B-C formation (labeled in blue) which eroded approximately 23.6% of the substantial bull campaign from the 2015 lows.

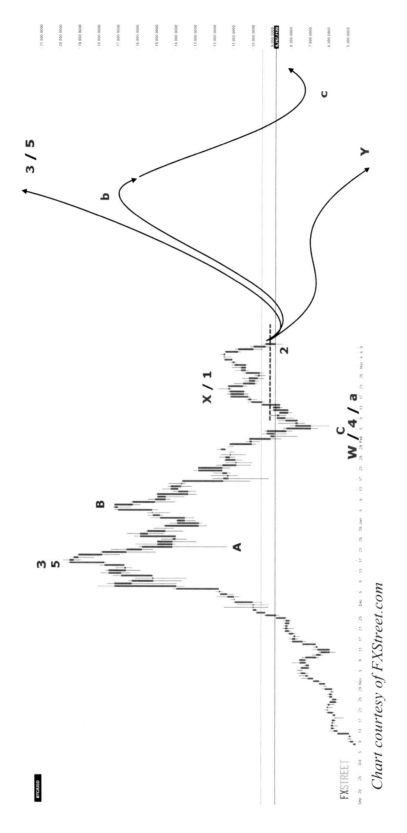

Chart courtesy of FXStreet.com

55

23.6% is one of the so-called "Fibonacci" ratios. Should this technical level be violated, the next destination, a 38.2% retracement, is to be found at 3,000 USD per Bitcoin.

The chart on the previous page shows three alternative Elliott Wave views of the Bitcoin price action.

The preferred view assumes a double zig-zag correction labeled W-X-Y (in red), which is now forming wave Y and thus calling for a deeper correction.

The second view assumes a finished wave 4 correction at approximately 5,900 and the potential for new high in a relatively short amount of time.

According to this more positive scenario, we are now starting wave 5 of major degree (in red), in which the impulsive recovery from the aforementioned low can be regarded as wave 1 (blue).

According to one of Elliott's basic rules, wave 2 of the same degree (in blue) should not overlap the termination of wave 1 (marked on the chart with an horizontal dashed red line), an affair unfolding as we write these lines in March, 2018.

Some of the other cryptocurrencies have unfolded higher from the same February lows, but similarly to Bitcoin, are equally in danger of overlapping their initial 1st wave upswings.

This would suggest that all cryptocurrencies are staging a so-called "pro-regressive" wave (i.e., any rising wave which occurs within a corrective wave of a greater degree) from February's lows, but as part of a complex correction. This complex correction can unfold in a W-X-Y formation as stated above, and has the potential to take the price even lower.

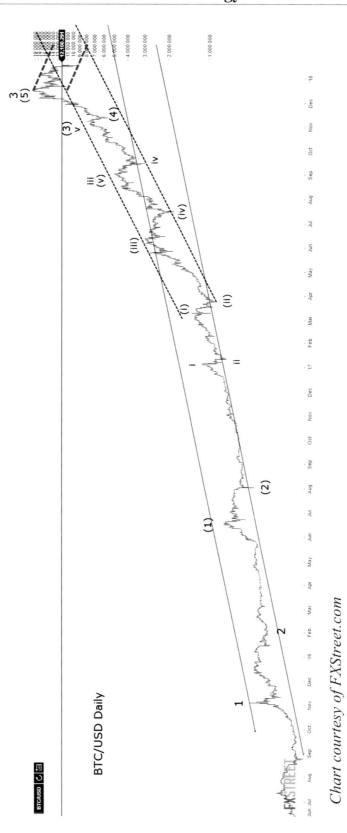

Chart courtesy of FXStreet.com

The other alternative view contemplates a formation of a triangle pattern which may not be so deep in terms of price correction, but which will potentially last longer – it could be several months in duration – prior to a breakout to higher highs.

Illustrating this particular view, we have labeled wave a and b (in red) as part of an uncompleted a-b-c-d-e triangle pattern (where waves a, c and e would establish support, while waves b and d would delimit resistance).

The Ratio scale chart that we presented on page 50 in the first part of this study merits reviewing again in order to contextualize the current Bitcoin correction within the bigger picture.

Elliott observed that impulse waves are usually limited in their advance by parallel support and resistance lines, forming price channels. Other analysts who followed Elliott also discovered that corrective waves are formed within channels, just like impulse waves.

Unlike the latter, corrective channels are less inclined than impulsive ones. Since price can not remain perpetually in a channel and needs to break out of it to enter into a trend and form an impulse wave, following this same logic, once the impulsive movement has finished, the price re-enters the impulsive channel confirming that a correction of the same cycle is in formation.

That is exactly what's happening right now in Bitcoin as well as in the majority of Crypto assets.

A hint that we are leaving the corrective mode would be a breakout of the declining channel (in dashed red) or a breakout from an eventual triangle, as mentioned in one of the deployed wave counts.

Point & Figure – The Ultimate Potential Price Targets

Because of the exceptionally strong Bitcoin rally in 2017, we have opted to assign a more or less liberal box size when constructing a Point and Figure chart.

In this case a 5% box size was used, this means each X and O is an advancement (or retracement) of 5% in the price of Bitcoin.

By doing so, we come up with a chart offering several so-called "counts" or price objectives.

Counts 1 and 2 have their origin in movements below 1,000 USD per Bitcoin. They, as well as count 3, drawn from an X column which started at 1,000 USD per Bitcoin, were all achieved between 2016 and 2017.

While most of the counts used in this chart are of a vertical nature, count 4 is an horizontal one.

This count suggested a potential move toward 900 USD per Bitcoin, but was quickly deactivated (see the dashed red line).

This rapid deactivation was triggered by a new up leg – an up leg which

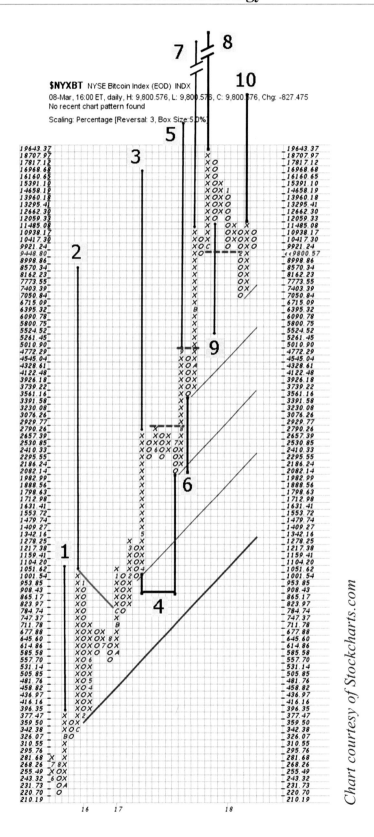

$NYXBT NYSE Bitcoin Index (EOD) INDX
08-Mar, 16:00 ET, daily, H: 9,800.576, L: 9,800.576, C: 9,800.576, Chg: -827.475
No recent chart pattern found

Scaling: Percentage [Reversal: 3, Box Size:5.0%]

Chart courtesy of Stockcharts.com

60

was designated for a mission to accomplish target count 5 towards 23,900. Target 5, in turn, was activated with the new up leg which paved the way for count 7, but left us with unfilled higher projections.

It's worth mentioning that this count would be invalidated with a price movement below 3,700. In between, count 6 was established but it required a new column of Os penetrating the 3,500 level to be activated, which did not happen.

The latest portion of the run-up phase created counts 7 and 8 and opened measured move objectives towards 103,000 and 72,500 respectively.

Before count 8 was deactivated, a new downside target emerged from a first column of Os after the all-time high, labeled count 9, targeting the 5,500 area.

The most recent count 10 threatens the mentioned downside target, but it does not invalidate it. Although count 10 returns focus to the December highs, it has been even lower than the previous ones, pointing squarely at 29,000.

Point and Figure counts work best when several box sizes can be used to find confluences between targets extracted from different charts.

Feel free to explore this century-old technique to find potential targets in Bitcoin.

Conclusions

From a pure charting perspective, Bitcoin must deal convincingly with the multiple downside obstacles, especially the one looming in the 7,700 range, and then sustain itself well above 12,000, in order to turn its technical status positive for 2018.

Further below on the price scale, between 2,000 and 3,000, we find another major support level which should act as a hindrance for an even deeper collapse in it price. This could be considered an exceptional bargain price for a long commitment.

If, in turn, you are a short-term oriented trader wanting to be in the market for quick profits while eliminating market risk, Momentum indicators can provide a signal when there is acceleration and a position entered has the potential to move into the green zone rapidly.

Right now Bitcoin is in a deceleration mode though, with the ROC indicator dipping below its zero-line. Waiting for a positive signal in the indicator is a prudent measure to undertake if you are planning to purchase Bitcoins.

I believe this intermediate bear market still has legs in it. It is recommended you hold your horses for a dip below 7,700 and then look to go long in intervals as Bitcoin eventually moves toward the 2,000-3,000 range.

From an Elliott Wave perspective, remember that it's not about finding the true wave structure, for there are most always several permutations in a given market following Elliott's rules and guidelines. The value of this Principle relies in having a more favorable picture of what the market is capable of doing.

In our case, from all three views examined, two of them are of corrective nature and just one points to a potential continuation of the rising trend. Be forewarned that corrective affairs are more difficult to trade and can drain your capital and patience. Be prepared for a meandering price action – perhaps for longer than you might desire – and control your gut reactions with Elliott Wave analysis.

From a Point and Figure perspective, we have a debilitating structure in terms of unfilled upside counts with the latest three targets decreasing in magnitude. Reaffirming the bearish view from the previous analysis, there is a new downside target threatening with a correction towards 5,800. Notice that this target would need a new all-time high to be invalidated!

Only an activation of the recent count from the February lows with a price surge above 12,000 would reduce the odds of a deeper correction. Another case for additional upward progress would be if the market fails to achieve the 5,500 area and stages a satisfactory reaction in the form of a new column of Xs.

Blockchain, Cryptocurrencies and The Planets

By Bill Meridian

The cryptocurrency mania raises the question as to which planetary phenomena are related to this development. Because Bitcoin has become so big so fast, there must be some major planetary configuration reflecting this event here on earth.

Having studied the Hamburg School, I had been awaiting the transit of the hypothetical planet, Apollon, into the money sign of Scorpio. Apollon is a benefic that rules widespread developments, science, and distribution. Whereas Jupiter rules "large," Apollon rules "many."

I have seen the horoscope of a book (Mercury) distributor (Apollon) who had Apollon/Mercury=MC. Also, a distributor of women's clothes had Venus/Apollon=MC.

A distributor of electronic gadgets had a horoscope chart with Pallas/Apollon=MC. Raven Star is one of the leading direct sales people in the USA, a frequent speaker at Tony Robbins seminars. She was born with an Ascendant, 0° Libra, Apollon conjunction.

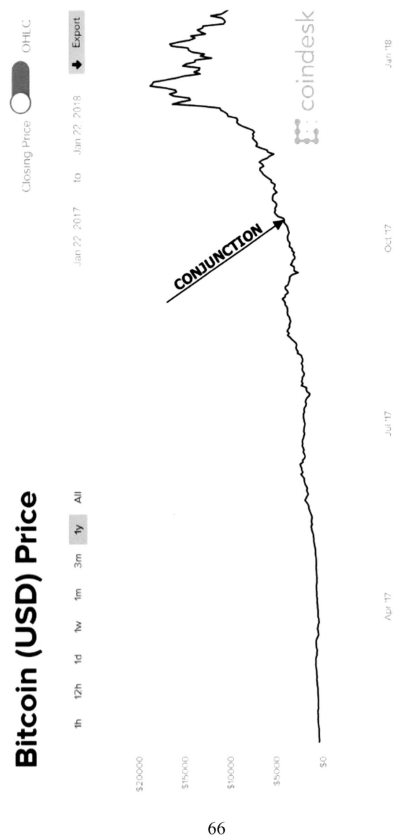

Price Chart Courtesy of Coindesk

In Alfred Witte's ***Rules for Planetary Pictures***, Apollon/Jupiter is described as "money in circulation." When we experienced Uranus=Jupiter/Apollon by transit in 2017, three countries announced changes in their money supply. India withdrew large bills from circulation suddenly, disrupting their economy. Saudi Arabia withdrew certain coins from circulation, and an African nation announced a future switch to a fully digital currency. As I noted in my book, ***Planetary Economic Forecasting***, all great free-market economists of the Austrian school have Jupiter and Apollon strong in their natal horoscopes.

I thought that the upcoming Jupiter-Apollon conjunction would accelerate the price of Bitcoin. It did so, as we can see in the graph on the previous page.

When Apollon entered Scorpio and Bernie Sanders began to mention "income redistribution," the connection was obvious.

I personally did not make the cryptocurrency-Apollon connection until the early autumn of 2017. There was a Mercury-Jupiter-Apollon conjunction at 1° Scorpio in mid-October, square my natal Jupiter at 1° Aquarius.

In October, I flew to the USA. On the Monday prior to departure, I met with my professor friends at the Vienna University of Business and Economics. They told me that they were starting a cryptocurrency department in 2018, likely the first such department at any university.

While in the USA, I attended a lecture by Professor David Yermack, NYU's expert in this area. First, I was amazed by the large numbers that he quoted concerning the companies that are hiring data experts and the magnitude of their move into this new field. Yermack explained that since 1850, the cost of transferring funds was about 2%. If any technology can reduce this percentage, it is of great interest to large institutions.

He stressed that the currencies themselves were not the big issue, but instead it was the blockchain technology that enables cryptos. As he described how the technology works, I made the connection to the Uranian planet

Admetos. Yermack said that each blockchain was unique and inviolate, both Admetos qualities. This planet also rules miniaturization. Admetos has just transited into Gemini. I had already made the connection of this sign change to speech restrictions and free speech zones. Yermack's description made the connection to blockchain.

Jupiter-Apollon Conjunction

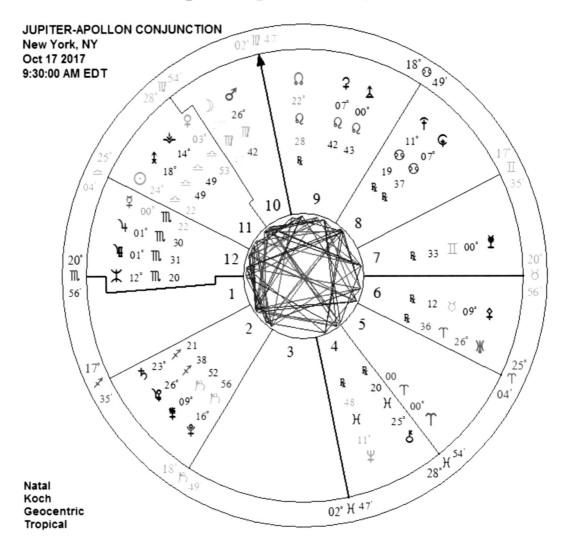

JUPITER-APOLLON CONJUNCTION
New York, NY
Oct 17 2017
9:30:00 AM EDT

Natal
Koch
Geocentric
Tropical

At this point, allow me to explain that these planets move very slowly, so the trends associated with them are not going to fade away overnight. In fact, the fastest Uranian planet moves at a rate of about 1° yearly.

Also, note below that Apollon and Admetos are 150° apart. On a 90° dial, we can see that the midpoint of the pair has been transiting back and forth over the World Point at 0° Aries. This is the planetary reason that cryptocurrencies and bitcoin have captured the public's attention.

Jupiter-Apollon Conjunction on a 90° Dial

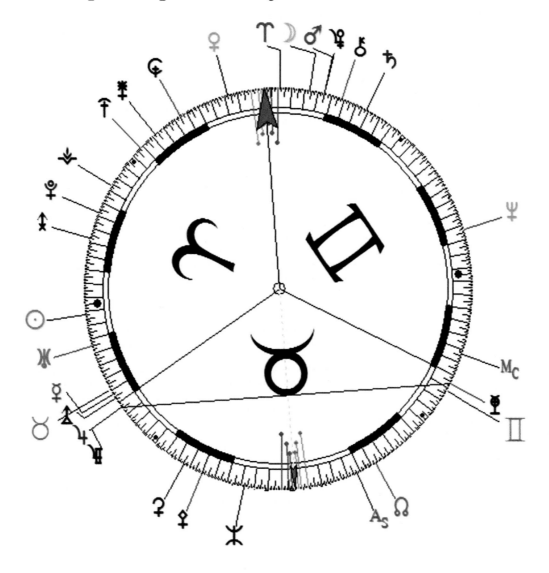

The Future of the Cryptocurrencies

I met with a member of the Mellon banking family in New York City two years ago. He was a backer of Bitcoin. He said that he had been contacted by the government and was planning to work with them to develop a government coin. One IT professional told me that a "US Coin" is under development.

My thought from the beginning was that this is too great an opportunity for the taxman to pass up. Control would enable the government to track all transactions and to catch tax evaders. I think that they will develop a cryptocurrency and will offer inducements that the private sector is unable to provide, such as assurances of safety and some regulation. This development is likely to put many of the less strong currencies out of business.

At the Ludwig Von Mises economic conference in New York City in October, 2017, I asked some of the professors to share their opinions about this new industry.

All agreed that cryptos are a medium of exchange, but do not fulfill all of the functions of a currency.

One person asked if these new currencies were inflationary, but another reminded us that the quantity of bitcoins was fixed. Another replied that many new such currencies were being created, and that this in itself might be inflationary.

My addition to the debate was to comment that this is a zero-sum game. If one buys a Bitcoin, one gives up the cash in exchange for the coin, as in the case of stock purchases. No new currency is created.

The number of Bitcoins, unlike federal reserve notes, is fixed. No wonder people want to exchange fed notes for Bitcoins!

Also, one must recall that at the beginning of any new business, such as the automobile industry, there is a rush into the field. In the early days, there were many car companies, and only a few remain. The same will happen with cryptos. The strong ones like Bitcoin and Ethereum are likely to survive, while the weaker, less well-managed cryptos will disappear.

Bitcoin on a 90° Dial

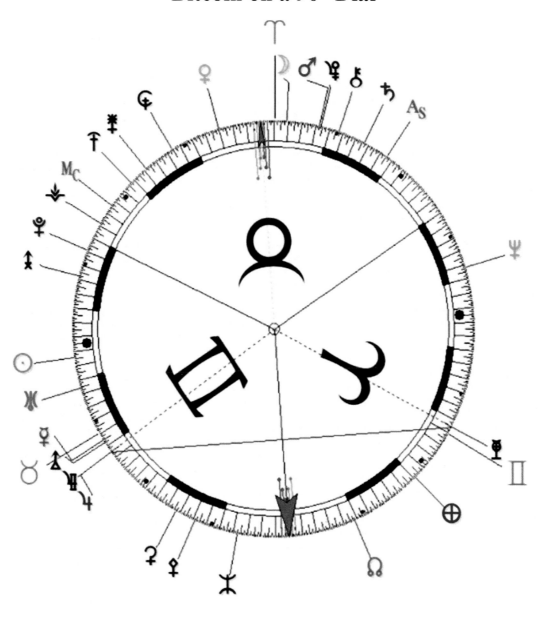

As to timing the Bitcoin price, I can only point to S-curves or Elliott Waves. In terms of the latter, it appears that Bitcoin is in the 3rd wave, the strongest of the 5-wave sequence. A wave 4 pullback follows, which where the cryptos are at the time of this writing in January, 2018. That wave 4 pullback is likely to end at 8,000-10,000. This will likely be followed by a wave 5 to a new all-time high before a serious correction starts. I do not know what the timing might be because we do not have enough data.

A Key to Personal Trading Timing

While I was finding the planetary pictures in the first-trade charts of stocks of companies that are related to blockchain, I noted that the picture Jupiter+Uranus-Apollon was strong.

I always note this picture when I set up a horoscope for the trading day in New York City. By transit, this point was moving over my natal Sun and Venus as my holdings in these stocks began a rapid appreciation. I suggest that traders watch this point on a 90° dial to determine how this transiting picture aspects their own natal planets.

Bitcoin Dates

Once enough dates relating to Bitcoin have been documented, one can enter them into a program to determine the all-important degree area. Here are some key dates that we have so far:

August 18, 2008: An unknown person or entity registered the bitcoin.org domain.

October 31, 2008: "Bitcoin: A Peer-To-Peer Electronic Cash System" was posted to a cryptography mailing list, published under the name "Satoshi Nakamoto". The whitepaper outlined the foundation of how bitcoin would operate.

January 3, 2009: The genesis block is mined. Block 0, the genesis block, is established at 18:15:05 GMT.

January 8, 2009: The first version of bitcoin is announced, and shortly thereafter, bitcoin mining begins.

January 12, 2009: The first bitcoin transaction. the first transaction of bitcoin currency, in block 170, takes place between Satoshi and Hal Finney, a developer and cryptographic activist.

October 5, 2009: An exchange rate is established.

May 22, 2010: 10,000 BTC is spent on pizza in Jacksonville, Florida. The first commercial transaction.

Five Astrological Approaches to Trading Bitcoin

Tim Bost

The astro-trading advantage has a lot to offer for active Bitcoin traders, and for longer-term investors as well, the so-called Bitcoin "HODLers". But the application of astrology to Bitcoin trading is not about using astrology in a vacuum; to be effective in market analysis and trading, astrology needs to be combined with technical analysis and an understanding of market fundamentals, whether we are looking at Bitcoin, the stock market, FOREX, or any other trading opportunity.

It's also important to recognize the fact that astrology can be a versatile tool in understanding the markets and in identifying potentially profitable opportunities. In fact, there are five key ways that we can apply astrological knowledge to trading Bitcoin. (Although we are focusing here primarily on the trading context, keep in mind that we can also employ these same concepts to help us evaluate longer-term positions as well.)

First of all, we can deal with transits to key horoscopes. In this approach we determine what the important horoscopes are that can potentially reflect an impact on Bitcoin, and then evaluate the potential effects from the current positions of the planets along the way, comparing the transiting positions to the positions and alignments in the base charts for Bitcoin.

Note that we're talking about "horoscopes" and "base charts" in the plural. As astrologers it's all too easy for us to fall into arguments about the single "true" or "correct" radix chart to use in our analysis, while putting on blinders so we can avoid looking at data that fails to confirm our own individual biases and preconceived notions about the way that the world is really supposed to be. But if we make an effort to keep our minds open, and if we are willing to consider multiple horoscopes as potentially valid radix charts receiving transits, we have much to gain. This is especially true when we are engaged in a new field of study like Bitcoin.

Secondly, we can use astrology to investigate trading opportunities in Bitcoin by looking at transit-to-transit dynamics. With this approach we can consider different planetary alignments, like a conjunction of Mars and Venus or the opposition of the Sun and Moon at the Full Moon, and look at what is happening with Bitcoin when those celestial events occur. But with this technique we're not talking about the transiting planetary dynamics relative to a base chart, like the chart we have decided best represents the inception of Bitcoin. We are only considering the current planetary dynamics in the sky, which is also a valid way of evaluating Bitcoin and its trading potential as well.

Especially as a follow-up to transit-to-transit observations, harmonic analysis is a third important method for applying astrological insights to Bitcoin or to other markets. Once we identify significant inflection points or strong trend reversals in the trading history of Bitcoin, we can look for the dominant planetary harmonic patterns that were present when those trading events occurred. By coordinating those planetary harmonics with price coordinates in the trading history, we can then project them into the future by using planetary price lines generated from upcoming planetary alignments, thereby informing our market expectations by establishing potential levels of trading support and resistance with an astrological basis.

In a fourth approach to using astrology in our analysis of trends and trading opportunities, we can also do studies of wave counts and vibrational analysis, using tools like Elliott Wave projections or Fibonacci retracements. Or we can use other methods of cycle analysis.

When we use this approach we can make an effort to find out the predominant cyclic vibrations in Bitcoin trading, as well as the typical duration of those cycles. Then we use that information as a springboard to look for astrological phenomena and coordinates that approximate those same cycles. If we discover a cycle that's evident in the trading environment, then maybe it's actually reflecting a planetary dynamic that's not readily apparent to us. If we can determine the existence of that cycle, and do some market back-testing to determine its reliability, then we can go back and superimpose the planetary interpretation on it, which can help us open up our awareness of new iterations of that cycle, and fine-tune our understanding of it along the way.

Finally, we can also look at astrological midpoints, as well as planetary pictures. Midpoints are simply the central point of location in celestial longitude between the positions of two planets. A planetary picture adds a third planet or significant horoscope point to the mix, so we're looking at slightly more complex arrangements of planetary symmetry, and sensitive angles of arc opening. This approach to using astrology in market analysis can often help us identify potential stress points and trading opportunities that we simply wouldn't be aware of otherwise.

Let's examine each of these five methodologies in greater detail, so that we can understand their differences – and so we can figure out ways of combining them for more effective analysis and Bitcoin forecasting.

1. Transits To A Radix Horoscope

The most common approach used by astrologers in forecasting is rooted in the examination of the position of transiting planets relative to a radix horoscope. That base chart, in the realm of natal astrology, is typically the birth chart of a particular individual. But in financial astrology, and in the effort to use astrological tools for financial analysis and market timing, there are a variety of horoscopes which can be used as radix charts, giving us a variety of potential reference points to consider in the light of current and future transits.

Some financial astrologers examine the charts of incorporation dates or the dates for the founding of companies, which can give us useful information about businesses in general. In the trading arena, however, the First-Trade horoscope has consistently proven to be the most valuable chart in revealing potential price fluctuations and profitable trading opportunities.

In the case of a publicly traded stock, the First-Trade date is the day that shares were first available for purchase through a public auction on an open market. It's worth remembering that the First-Trade date is often different than the date for an IPO, which is sometimes a closed affair with shares offered only to pre-subscribed investors and fund managers with direct associations to the underwriters of the public offering.

While some financial astrologers go to extreme means in an effort to determine the precise timing of the market transactions in which orders for newly-listed shares were first filled and recorded, practical experience has shown that useful trading information can be gleaned from First-Trade horoscopes which conform to the standards expressed by George Bayer in the

1940s and later articulated by Bill Meridian in his more recent work on planetary stock trading.

This approach times the First-Trade horoscope by the opening bell on the stock exchange, rather than by the precise timing of an actual transaction. The notion behind this method is that no matter when transactions actually occur, the stock is theoretically available at the time that the exchange opens, so the opening bell marks a significant event in the life of that security.

With Bitcoin, of course, we are dealing with a market entity that has primarily operated largely outside the realm of regulated bourses and well-established exchanges for securities transactions. It is not a simple matter to determine which of the many Bitcoin horoscopes is the most appropriate to use as a radix chart for forecasting and future speculation. At this early stage in the history of Bitcoin and of Bitcoin astrology, this approach is simply one of trial and error, examining various radix charts, formulating hypotheses about future trends, back-testing previous market performance with reference to the transiting aspects, and then seeing how well price movements actually coincide with our astrological projections.

As we are doing this trial and error analysis, it's again helpful to remember that the goal is not to come up with an unequivocal either/or decision about the One True Horoscope which best represents Bitcoin and its potential. Sometimes it's wise to include key points from multiple charts in order to get a more complete picture of the possibilities. If, for example, we are looking at a particular event in cyberspace that occurred at a precisely-documented time, but for which the location is uncertain, we may have several horoscopes with identical planetary placements, but with different chart angles. By choosing one of those charts as a base, and by then adding the chart angles from the other horoscopes as sensitive points within that base chart, we can come up with a combination that keeps us open to multiple possibilities as we explore transiting factors and their potential correlation to market events.

The need for back-testing cannot be overemphasized. If, for example, we are looking at an upcoming date when transiting Mars will conjoin Jupiter in a potential radix chart that we are considering, we may have strong feelings about what this alignment will portend for Bitcoin prices at that time. But we can speculate with a much higher degree of confidence if we go back and examine all of the previous examples from past Mars transits to that Jupiter point, and take note of the ways that Bitcoin prices actually reacted under those circumstances.

To be even more thorough in our investigation, it's a good idea to examine the dates of key trend reversals in Bitcoin trading, those times when the fluctuating prices hit significant highs or lows and then changed direction. On those occasions, what were the transiting planets doing to the radix chart that we are currently considering? If we don't see key correlations between planetary alignments and significant price movements, then we may want to continue searching elsewhere for appropriate radix horoscopes.

As far as back-testing is concerned, there are some key considerations which we must keep in mind. Most importantly, we must have sufficient price history to give us the data that we need in order to reach conclusions about planetary movements and their coordination with market timing. If we only have one or two previous examples of a particular planetary alignment having occurred during the price history that we have available, then it's not particularly useful for us to draw conclusions about its implications for possible future outcomes. But if we have several dozen examples of a particular planetary alignment having occurred, then we can be far more confident in using it as a basis for our forecasts.

There's an obvious corollary here. If we are to determine which active forces emanating from celestial alignments can give us legitimate clues about future price fluctuations, then our bias will be more toward the faster-moving planets which have repeatedly transited the radix horoscope we are considering. While transiting Pluto crossing the Midheaven of a radix chart may give us compelling ideas about potential price ramifications, this slow-moving alignment offers us little opportunity for meaningful back-testing and, except perhaps for the occurrence of one or two iterations due to retrograde motion.

As a practical rule, it's most useful to have at least seven years of price history in hand before we begin to speculate about the effects of upcoming transits to any radix horoscope in the financial markets. This Seven Year Rule of Thumb has a correlation to approximately one-fourth of a Saturn cycle. If we have enough price history in hand to be able to examine what has transpired when transiting Saturn has come to a square to its position in the radix horoscope, then we can operate with a higher level of certainty about our observations and assumptions.

Based on this Seven Year Rule of Thumb, we are only now coming into the time when we can begin to examine Bitcoin horoscopes as potential radix charts in measuring the impact of transiting planetary alignments. This same rule also makes it clear that we would be premature in any effort to apply this transit-to-radix astrological methodology to some of the newer cryptocurrencies, which have much shorter price histories.

For that matter, because the trading history of Bitcoin itself is still quite brief, we still have relatively few iterations of transiting phenomena to rely on as we try to understand planetary effects from the past and back-test the market performance of Bitcoin as various planetary alignments impacted the radix charts we are considering. So at this stage of the game, drawing conclusions about the real influence of planetary transits on Bitcoin prices, and then forecasting future trends on that basis, is a tenuous proposition at best.

Even so, it's an activity well worth pursuing, especially if we look at examinations of transits to Bitcoin horoscopes as a pioneering, somewhat experimental investigation. We can at least begin to lay the groundwork for future astrological inquires based on more accumulated market data. And as we develop and refine our methodologies for astrological Bitcoin analysis, it's just as helpful to know what doesn't work as it is to discover reliable planetary signatures for Bitcoin price movements.

For example, the Bitcoin Proposal horoscope for Satoshi Nakamoto's publication of the Bitcoin white paper has not proven to be particularly effective in forecasting the Bitcoin market. It is a profoundly significant horoscope, especially in our understanding of the philosophical and conceptual foundations of Bitcoin. Transits to it, particularly transits from solar eclipses, have revealed useful insights into the shifting social acceptance and geopolitical implications of Bitcoin. But based on our studies so far, transits to this particular horoscope do not seem to correlate very well with major moves in the price of Bitcoin.

Or consider the horoscope for the Bitcoin Genesis Block, when Satoshi performed the first transaction with Bitcoin to document it as an active entity, creating the first block in what was to rapidly become the Bitcoin blockchain. Every subsequent transaction in the blockchain ultimately goes back to this originating one, which was the first block of data validating the transmission of Bitcoin as a mathematical quality from one encrypted online address to another. It's obviously an extremely important horoscope in the history of Bitcoin.

Some sources record this Bitcoin Genesis Block event as taking place on January 4, 2009 at 3:15 a.m. Japan Standard Time in Tokyo, Japan. But we also have a chart for the Bitcoin Genesis Block that is set for Sydney, Australia on January 3 instead of January 4. And when we examine the Sydney chart in detail, we can observe that for some reason the time of the event has been noted in Greenwich Mean Time instead of Australian time.

A closer look at these two horoscopes reveals an intriguing fact. Although they are nominally set for two different days, both charts show the Moon at precisely the same zodiacal position – 4°33' Aries! These two horoscopes are, in fact, the same chart – or at least they are both horoscopes for precisely the same moment in time, recorded in two different locations. The discrepancy is compounded by the event's proximity to midnight and by the fact that one of the two charts has been recorded in GMT instead of local standard time, causing a shift to a different date on the calendar.

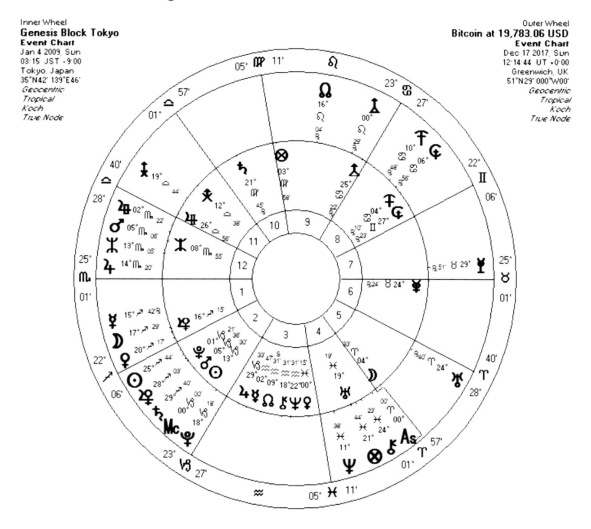

As an example of using transit-to-radix dynamics, let's compare the Tokyo Genesis Block chart as a base horoscope with the transiting planetary configurations at the time of the Bitcoin record high on December 17, 2017. By focusing on this historic event in the life of Bitcoin, we should be able to see some noteworthy planetary correspondences.

The inner circle is the chart for the Tokyo Genesis Block, which we are comparing to the chart for the positions of the transiting planets on December 17, 2017, when we hit the all-time trading high – that's the chart shown in the outer ring. The first thing we note here is the position of transiting Jupiter, because it's making a very significant alignment, a waning sextile to the Genesis Block Sun, with Jupiter at 14° Scorpio and the radix Sun at 13° Capricorn to create a 60° angle between the two. Symbolically, of course, Jupiter represents expansion, while the Sun is the integrity and basic vitality of Bitcoin itself, so this gives us an interesting indication of the potential for a trading high.

We should note here that the Jupiter cycle runs about 12 years, and this alignment of transiting Jupiter to the Genesis Block Sun took place roughly nine years after the Genesis Block event. So this was first and only time in the history of Bitcoin that this particular waning sextile alignment had occurred. The next time it will happen will be in late November and early December, 2029.

At the same time as this particular alignment of transiting Jupiter in 2017, however, we note that transiting Mars is at 5° Scorpio. This transiting Mars position is also interesting because of its 60° alignment with the Genesis Block Mars at 5° Capricorn – at the time of the record high price for Bitcoin, we thus had Mars sextile Mars, as well as Jupiter sextile the Sun. This is symbolically a remarkable configuration because Jupiter has to do with the expansion of Bitcoin's value, while the Mars/Mars activation is an appropriate depiction of the wild trading peak creating a trading top after what was essentially a perpendicular or parabolic move to the upside. It was, of course, followed by an equally precipitous decline.

We can note as well that transiting Mars is also in a trine to the transneptunian factor Kronos in the Genesis Block horoscope. Kronos represents the highest high, or the greatest possible heights, so this is a very direct planetary indication of Bitcoin hitting what has been its all-time high so far.

On top of that, Mars continues its activating influence of the Genesis Block chart, forming a quincunx, a 150° angle, to the Genesis Block Moon. The Moon moves very rapidly and is an indicator of constantly changing public moods, so this Mars trigger indicates a spike in public awareness of Bitcoin, with the potential for a major shift in the general perception of the cryptocurrency.

In keeping with that assessment of public opinion about Bitcoin, it's noteworthy as well that transiting Chiron is in a semi-square to the True North Lunar Node in the Genesis Block horoscope. This suggests that while the news of the Bitcoin record high was compelling and somewhat controversial, it was also likely to have the net positive effect of encouraging more people to connect with the cryptocurrency.

Finally, we shouldn't overlook the role of transiting Venus at the time of the trading top. Venus, at 20° Sagittarius, is square the Genesis Block Uranus at 19° Pisces. The Venus/Uranus combination is often significant in financial astrology. Venus signifies things which are pleasing, beautiful and refined, while Uranus is the planet of explosions and surprises. As in this case, when the two planets get together, things can start to look surprisingly good!

Even with this cursory look at transits to the Genesis Block chart, when we add all these factors together there's clearly quite an impact. And when we are looking at the transits to a key horoscope, we can do so on a long-term basis or on a short-term basis. We can look at the transits to a radix chart over an extended period of time and anticipate what might happen when Saturn crosses the Midheaven, five years from now. We can gain much richer insights into the potential for changes in the price over an extended period, and we can apply the same technique to shorter-term time horizons as well. In other words, this traditional approach to financial astrology certainly shouldn't be abandoned, in spite of our occasional concerns about the nuances of the radix charts we are considering.

2. Transiting Planets To Transiting Planets

As an example for transit-to-transit dynamics as a tool for understanding price fluctuations in Bitcoin, we will once again use the record high horoscope for December 17, 2017. Note that the chart is set for Universal Time at the Greenwich Meridian, which is the standard we are using for cyberspace horoscopes without specific local points of reference.

This is a remarkable horoscope. The first thing that commands our attention is that the chart, timed for the intraday trading peak for Bitcoin on the date of its record high, features the 0° point of the four cardinal signs of the zodiac on the chart angles, the cusps of the first, fourth, seventh, and tenth houses. That's a striking indication that we are dealing with an event of global significance.

Saturn is especially prominent by virtue of its conjunction with the Midheaven (this record-breaking event took place just 36 hours before Saturn's ingress into Capricorn. This position gives us a hint of Saturn's role in limiting the upward move in the price of Bitcoin. Remember that a trading top is just that – it marks the time when we can expect lower prices ahead.

Even so, the dominant planetary pattern in this horoscope is the Water Grand Trine featuring Neptune in Pisces, Kronos in Cancer, and the Jupiter/Poseidon conjunction in Scorpio. This is a configuration that provides the perfect picture of achieving new heights of abundance in ways that stir the imagination. But due to Neptune dissipating energy, it also indicates the likelihood that those new heights will soon recede.

The Mercury trine with the True Lunar Node reveals the ease with which the concept of Bitcoin's hitting new highs can foster connections and conversations, but with Mercury in retrograde motion those conversations are likely to be ill-informed at best.

With Mars, the ruler of both the Ascendant and the financial eighth house, serving as the final planetary dispositor in the chart, the motivation for active trading is readily evident. But Mars is also in a trine to Hades, so this energetic market situation can easily get corrupted.

Overall the picture is one of an extremely dramatic situation. But note that the planetary alignments prominent in the horoscope, with their emphasis on outer planets and slow-moving configurations, are not likely to repeat with any frequency. So this kind of analysis may ultimately have limited value as a guideline for forecasting Bitcoin prices.

But our analysis of transit-to-transit dynamics is not limited to an examination of the horoscope wheel. It's also helpful to use the 45° graphic ephemeris as a tool for detecting transiting alignments, and for understanding their potential impact on trading activity.

The graphic ephemeris presents zodiacal positions in overlaid 45° increments, with 0° degrees of the cardinal signs at the top of the diagram extending to 15° of the fixed signs at the bottom, and then continuing with an overlay of 15° fixed at the top, extending to 30° mutable at the bottom. The ongoing positions of transiting planets are graphed from left to right, with the diagram becoming a calendar of specified duration. As these planetary lines move from left to right, they also simultaneously have a trajectory from the top of the diagram towards the bottom if they are in direct motion. On the other hand, if the lines moving left to right are moving from the bottom of the diagram toward the top, it's an indication that the designated planet is in retrograde motion at the time.

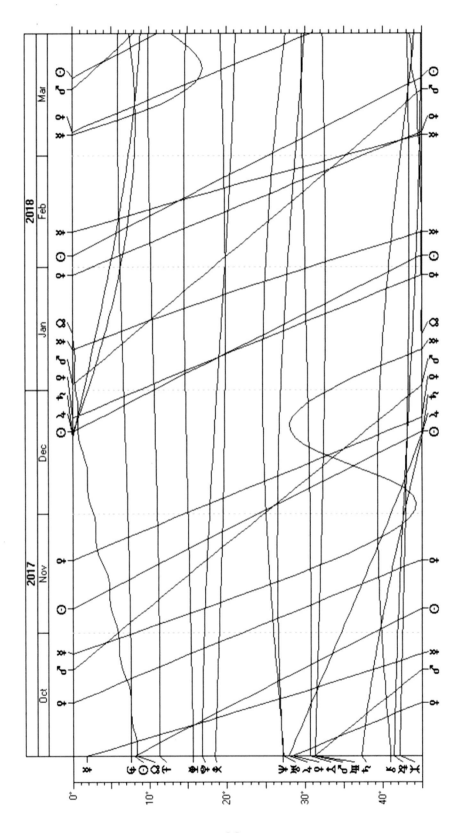

One benefit of the graphic ephemeris is that it can allow us to see an extended period of time and the planetary interactions contained within it in a single glance, giving us a powerful overview of long-term astrological potentials. We use the graphic ephemeris a lot in our financial astrology work because it helps us see durations of planetary events as well as the points of exact alignment. In traditional astrology a lot of emphasis is placed on the exact alignments, but in practical experience two planets can sometimes be in close angular proximity for somewhat extended periods of time. We can identify the whole time frame with this kind of diagram.

In addition to that, as in the case of the action surrounding the Bitcoin trading top, we can also zoom in on a specific portion of the graphic ephemeris to see key planetary interactions. Wherever there is a crossing of two planetary lines, it is an indication that there is an eighth-harmonic alignment between those planets. The eighth-harmonic aspects in traditional astrology are the conjunction, the opposition, the square, the semi-square, and the sesquiquadrate. These are the aspects that are the most likely to manifest as external, observable events, rather than as psychological nuances or as vague general trends.

The 45° graphic ephemeris shown on the previous page is a chart for the closing three months of 2017 and the opening three months of 2018, allowing us to see a six-month calendar that features all of the geocentric transiting positions of the planets and the transneptunian factors. Note, however, that even though this is a geocentric representation, the Moon has been left out of this chart. The Moon moves so rapidly through the zodiac that adding its transit lines makes the graphic ephemeris unnecessarily busy, complicating our ability to use it for helpful information.

While an examination of this six-month diagram gives us a good perspective on the flow of planetary energy and the points of maximum stress during the period that is shown, since we are primarily concerned with the action surrounding the trading high in Bitcoin, let's zoom in on the section of the chart that coincides with December, focusing on the lower half of the diagram, where we see the greatest concentration of planetary line crossings. For easier reference, we have labeled the lines on this enlarged presentation.

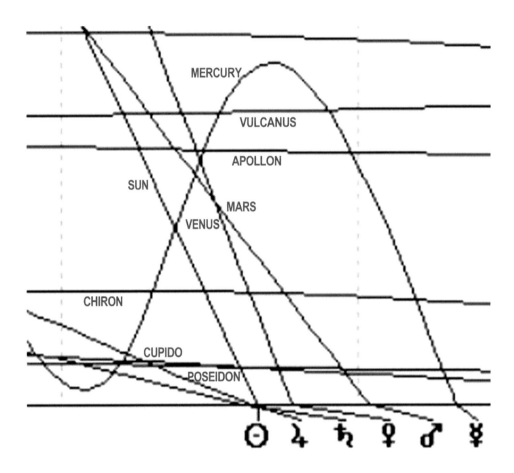

By using this tool, we can detect several key events that took place around the time of the trading high on December 17, 2017. Just prior to that date, there were eighth-harmonic alignments between Mercury and Venus, between Mercury and Apollon, and between the Sun and Chiron. On the exact date of the trading high there were eighth-harmonic interactions between Venus and Mars and between Mercury and Vulcanus. And throughout this critical time frame, there was also an extended tight alignment between the transneptunian factors Cupido and Poseidon.

In each case, these were planetary aspects that we might otherwise have missed, if we had relied only on a perusal of the horoscope wheel for this event. But the graphic ephemeris doesn't tell us exactly what aspects were involved; it only indicates eighth-harmonic alignments in a generic sense. Upon further investigation, we can see that the key planetary events surrounding the record trading top in Bitcoin were more specifically a Mercury/Venus conjunction, a Mercury/Apollon waxing semi-square, a Sun/Chiron waning square, a Venus/Mars waxing semi-square, a Mercury/Vulcanus waxing sesquiquadrate, and a Cupido/Poseidon waxing semi-square.

Note that even though some of the slow-moving transneptunian factors are included here, in most of these alignments there are also faster-moving planets involved. This means that we can use these active aspects as starting hypotheses for back-testing against the historical price data for Bitcoin, and perhaps discover correspondences which could prove valuable in forecasting.

And what does that back-testing show? To start with, we ignore the Cupido/Poseidon aspect, since it's so rare that it's impossible to back-test. And when we dig more deeply into these planetary alignments at the Bitcoin record high in December 2017, we learn that not all of them give us information that can inform our trading decisions with sufficient probability. That's the point of back-testing – to discover what really works, and what doesn't!

For example, our investigation of previous Sun/Chiron waning squares reveals that these particular planetary alignments are totally inconclusive in predicting Bitcoin trading tops. Based on the six previous examples in our trading history, this aspect has a precise 50-50 chance of indicating a Bitcoin price peak – not the kind of probability that we would want to risk any money on in a trading situation! This aspect will come up again on December 19, 2018; December 23, 2019; December 26, 2020; and December 29, 2021.

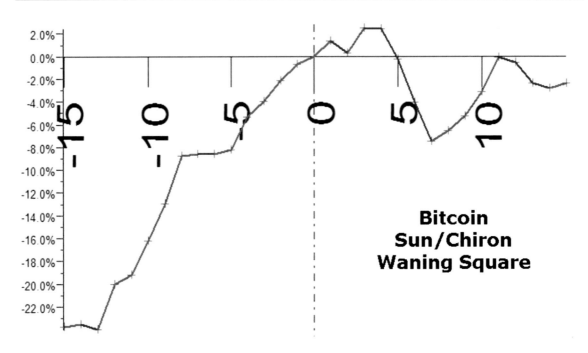

Our chart for this aspect shows the net average effect that it has had on the price of Bitcoin in the past. The vertical dotted line in the center of the chart represents the date of the aspect itself, with the average price changes shown for 15 days before and after the exact planetary alignment.

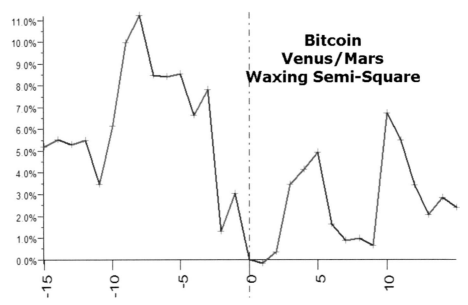

Venus/Mars waxing semi-squares are even worse as indicators of Bitcoin trading tops, based on five previous examples. They have accurately identified Bitcoin highs just 40% of the time. Because Mars take two years to transit the zodiac, these are fairly infrequent aspects – the next ones arrive on November 7, 2019; October 6, 2021; and December 27, 2021.

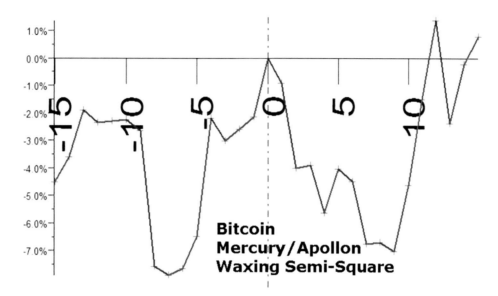

Mercury/Apollon waxing semi-squares are a bit more reliable, with 62.5% of the previous eight examples bringing Bitcoin prices lower. The next examples of this aspect will come on December 27, 2018; December 21, 2019; December 13, 2020; and December 7, 2021.

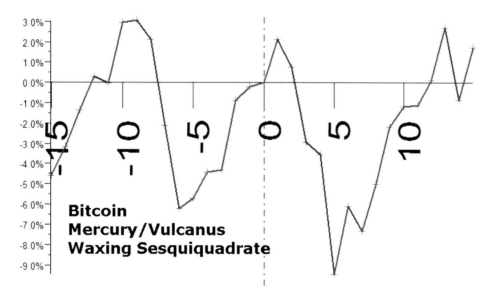

The Mercury/Vulcanus waxing sesquiquadrate, a 135° alignment, also has a 62.5% probability of coinciding with Bitcoin trading tops, based on eight previous occurrences. This planetary aspect will repeat on December 31, 2018; December 25, 2019; December 17, 2020; and October 10, 2021.

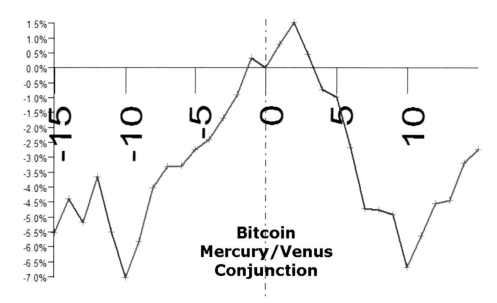

Of all the planetary alignments that we observed in our transit-to-transit analysis of the December 2017 trading high, Mercury/Venus conjunctions show the greatest correlation with significant trading tops in the price action for Bitcoin. Based on 14 previous iterations, this planetary alignment has a 71.4% probability of identifying a market high for Bitcoin. And it happens with some frequency; the next occurrences will be on October 15, 2018; July 24, 2019; September 13, 2019; October 30, 2019; May 22, 2020; February 23, 2021; April 25, 2021; May 29, 2021; and December 29, 2021.

The virtue of examining transit-to-transit planetary phenomena at times corresponding with key market movements is that this method sidesteps all the questions and concerns about having the right base horoscope for transit-to-radix analysis.

In practical experience, we can get the best results as financial astrologers when we use a combination of some or all of the approaches we are outlining here, so the transit-to-transit methodology is not necessarily meant as a substitute for transit-to-radix analysis. But there are certain times, especially when there's some lack of clarity about the appropriate data to use in a radix horoscope, when the tools of transit-to-transit analysis become extremely important.

3. Harmonic Analysis and Price Projection

We can amplify the results of our transit-to-transit analysis when we apply harmonic tools to our core understanding of Bitcoin trading dynamics. Harmonics are a way of describing the spatial relationships and energetic resonances between planets and other sensitive points in the horoscope. They are derived from sequences of vibratory expression, which can take many forms, perhaps most commonly in the sine wave and its variations.

In astrology, we primarily consider harmonics within the context of divisions of a circle's 360 degrees. The Ptolemaic aspects of traditional astrology are all strong, simple harmonic representations: the conjunction is the division of 360° by zero, giving us the first harmonic. The opposition, a 180° alignment which divides 360° by 2, represents the second harmonic. The trine, dividing 360° by 3 into 120° slices, creates the third harmonic. We get the square, a fourth-harmonic alignment, when we divide 360° by 4 to get 90° increments. And the sextile connects us with the sixth harmonic through dividing 360° by 6 to produce 60° increments.

In modern astrology we expand that traditional choir of aspects and include other harmonics in our calculations as well: the fifth harmonic (72°), the eighth harmonic (45°), the ninth harmonic (40°), the tenth harmonic (36°), the twelfth harmonic (30°), the fifteenth harmonic (24°), the eighteenth harmonic (20°), the twentieth harmonic (18°), and the twenty-fourth harmonic (15°), to name a few.

Harmonic studies can help us get a clearer and richer appreciation of the core structure and delicate nuances expressed through traditional planetary aspects and alignments. They can also reveal hidden energetic patterns in transit-to-transit events.

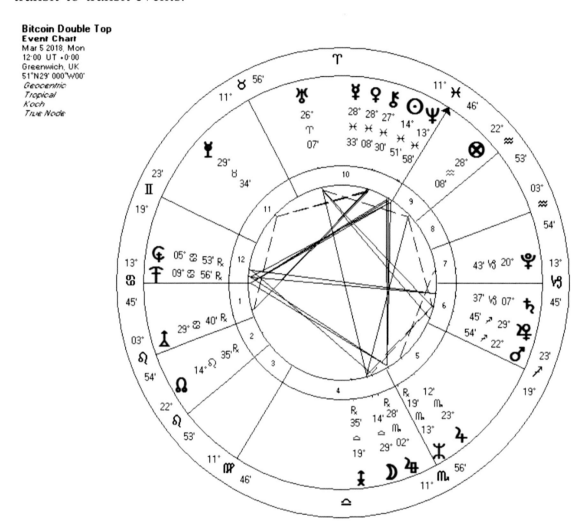

For example, when Bitcoin completed a double-top technical pattern on March 5, 2018 by failing to break through the price resistance at 11,802.23 set on February 20 and then hitting an intraday high of just 11,694.15 to trigger a sharp sell-off in the cryptocurrency, the horoscope for that trading day provided plenty of indicators of the potential for a trend reversal. They included a Sun/Neptune conjunction (feeling cheated, swindled or deluded); a

Moon/Uranus opposition (a sudden shift in sentiment); a Saturn/Kronos opposition (coming to a halt after hitting a peak), and a Mercury/Venus conjunction, which, as we have already seen, has a powerful track record as an indicator of Bitcoin trading tops.

But an examination of the harmonic structure of this event reveals that there was an unusually strong emphasis on the sixth harmonic at the time. In fact, nearly 45% of the planetary aspects in effect were associated with the sixth harmonic, including 16 trines and 9 sextiles, as well as 9 conjunctions and 3 oppositions. This hidden structure reinforces notions of a static situation in which unconscious biases become an inhibiting factor, opening the door to the possibility of emphatically negative expressions. This awareness of the sixth harmonic focus also calls attention to the planets included in the Grand Trine pattern created by Kronos, Poseidon, and the conjunction of the Sun and Neptune, as well as the strong inhibiting influence of Admetos in its sixth-harmonic alignments to Vulcanus and the Mercury/Venus conjunction.

And the practical usefulness of harmonics doesn't stop there. We can also use harmonic alignments as a keynote in defining the essential nature of trend reversals and pivot points in the trading history for Bitcoin, and then use that analysis as a basis for forecasting future trends.

As an example of this kind of approach, we can consider the important trading low in Bitcoin on February 6, 2018. Without referring to a radix horoscope of any kind, we can simply review the dominant planetary aspects that occurred on that date, and select one that includes both a fast-moving and a slower-moving object, to get a more dynamic picture of a potential trigger of the trend change. One of the most striking aspects on that date was a 135° sesquiquadrate (sometimes referred to as a sesquisquare) between Venus and the transneptunian factor Kronos. In the example shown on the following page, we've used the aspect identification module in the Fibonacci Trader – Galactic Trader software to help us spot this alignment more easily.

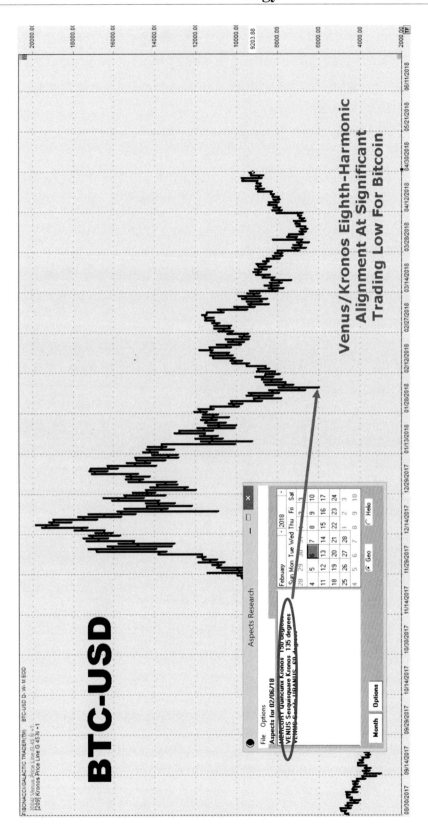

Note that the 135° sesquiquadrate between Venus and Kronos is an eighth-harmonic alignment. Based on years of experience and back-testing, we have found that eighth-harmonic aspects tend to be the most common harmonic energies that find expression in active trading, so it's not too unusual to see this in play at the time of trend reversal like this one.

The combination of Venus and Kronos is particularly useful here because Venus, with an orbital period of 224.65 days, moves much, much more rapidly that Kronos, a Kuiper Belt object with an orbital period of 521 years. This contrast means that the action of Kronos on market trends is more likely to be expressed as an undertone or standing wave, with very little short-term fluctuation, while Venus provides more frequent accent points to help shift short-term trading dynamics. Eighth-harmonic Venus/Kronos alignment occur approximately once every five weeks.

As a side note, we should acknowledge the fact that it's tempting to overlay symbolic interpretations of the planets at this point. After all, Venus is one of the traditional "money planets" and Kronos has symbolic connections with extraordinary highs, in or out of the market. So what could be more appropriate than this particular combination of planets in signaling a key shift in trading trend?

But even though that kind of imaginative speculation can be quite entertaining, with this approach to using astrology in the markets it's much better not to succumb to the temptation. We'll avoid symbolic thinking for the time being, and simply focus on the practical implications of this eighth-harmonic planetary connection in helping us project future trading trends.

The tools that we use for that kind of harmonic forecasting are planetary price lines. As explained in the book *Gann Secrets Revealed volume I*, there are specific relationships between planetary positions in celestial longitude and potential price levels in the markets. Those connections can be illuminated and amplified through the use of factoring and harmonic projections.

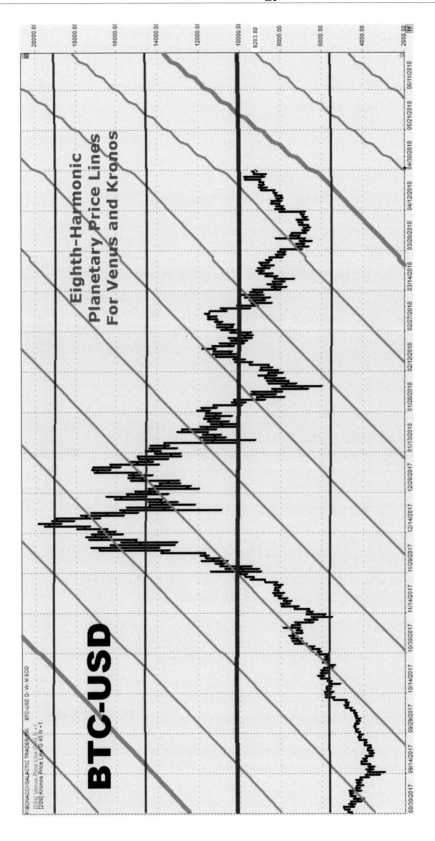

And because planetary positions change over time, we can take a "connect the dots" approach and convert those positions in celestial longitude into extended lines, for a representation that gives us a continuum of prices and trends established by the planets themselves – for any time frame in the past, or, even more importantly for our ability to forecast Bitcoin trends, for any time frame in the future as well.

We turn once again to the Fibonacci Trader – Galactic Trader software as our tool of choice for calculating these planetary price lines. In the chart shown on the previous page, we have added eighth-harmonic planetary price lines for geocentric Venus and Kronos. The positions of Kronos are represented here by the purple, more horizontal lines on the chart, while Venus positions are shown by the green, more diagonal lines.

In each case, the thicker lines for the planetary positions show first-harmonic alignments over time, while the thinner parallel lines are eighth-harmonic increments derived from those first-harmonic positions. Because these planetary price lines are projected in the eighth harmonic, the lines are each 45 "points" apart (360/8=45). With our presentation scaled to the current price range for Bitcoin, this means that the roughly horizontal Kronos lines are each $4,500.00 apart on the chart.

Adding these planetary price lines to our trading chart gives us a quick picture of the underlying structure of the trading action in Bitcoin, especially as it reflects longer-term market cycles. While the trading prices don't necessarily hug the planetary price lines, it's nevertheless clear that we can get a useful projection of trends and potential trading channels from observing the Venus lines. We can use the Kronos lines to help us watch for potential support and resistance zones of major significance.

The essential notion in this approach to applying astrology to the analysis of Bitcoin trading action is the realization that we can refine our astro-trading strategies by starting with the trading action at key inflection points or reversals, then determining the specific planets that were active at that time. Once we have made that determination, we examine the dominant harmonic relationships and then use them to derive our forecasts and projections of future trading behavior.

4. Planetary Correlations To Observed Waves and Cycles

When we look at waves and cycles as potential springboards for astrological trading analysis, we begin our inquiry from a radically different viewpoint. In this fourth approach to combining astrological perspectives and more conventional approaches to the markets, we don't start with a look at a radix horoscope, or even a representation of transit-to-transit dynamics. Instead, we use of the tools of technical analysis and the trading history available to us.

Technical analysis offers us a wonderful variety of powerful tools to use in that examination. As Gonçalo Moreira and other expert market technicians have discovered, Elliott Wave projections and Fibonacci Ratio retracements can give us some remarkable insights into potential Bitcoin trading action. By using tools like these, along with other techniques for cycle analysis, it's possible to discover useful patterns in Bitcoin trading activity, or at least to come up with reasonable assumptions about how the price of Bitcoin is likely to behave as particular cycles repeat themselves.

As astro-traders and financial astrologers, however, we don't stop with the determination of market-derived cycles alone. Once we have found a high-probability trading cycle based on market back-testing, we then examine that cycle in the light of potential correspondences with planetary phenomena. By looking for those correlations, we can often open up a richer understanding of underlying cycles in the market, and then move more confidently into research that is solidly based in the foundations of real astrology. That powerful combination gives us a remarkable opportunity to refine our forecasts and trading expectations.

As we begin to use this approach, however, it's best if we start from a purely technical frame of mind, once again setting aside our awareness of astrological symbolism for the time being. As many non-astrological traders know, we have already begun to understand some of the trading cycles at work with Bitcoin.

In fact, empirical analysis of the trading history of Bitcoin evaluated per the U.S. dollar (BTC-USD) reveals that about a dozen strongly-defined cycles can be detected in the trading action for the cryptocurrency. These cycles range from 8.7 days to 228 days.

The trading action in Bitcoin moves fast, and it's not unusual to see daily price swings that are equivalent to yearly changes in major market indices like the S&P 500. While the "year for a day" analogy may stretch the credulity of some seasoned traders who are used to multiple time frame analysis, it's nevertheless appropriate in the fast-paced world of Bitcoin and cryptocurrency speculation in general.

It's interesting to note that the cycles of shorter duration can be especially significant in effective analysis of this extremely volatile market. They can, in fact, provide some useful guidelines for short-term speculators seeking ways of capitalizing on the radical price swings which are so often expressed in the trading action for Bitcoin.

At the other extreme, however, efforts to understand the longer-term cycle dynamics of Bitcoin trading are much more tenuous. With less than ten years of Bitcoin trading history as a frame of reference, conclusions drawn from observations of longer-duration cycles in Bitcoin price action are necessarily much more tentative, and thus offer little certainty as forecasting tools.

While they may meet the minimum requirements for statistical significance, they ultimately seem to bring a negligible advantage to intermediate-term position players in the cryptocurrency.

As trading in Bitcoin continues to progress during the coming years, however, we will be able to add more empirical data to our research, and will thus be able to refine our understanding of the underlying cyclic nature of the volatility in this cryptocurrency. In the meantime, however, what should we be taking into consideration as we look for useful models and guidelines in trading Bitcoin?

The answer to that question may lie in the unique connections between cycle analysis and the remarkable perspectives provided by the astro-trading advantage. At least, that's certainly the bias that's presented in the pages of this book!

Especially as we engage in dialogue with the mainstream trading community, we as astrologers and astro-traders should remember that when we apply our knowledge of planetary cycles to the markets, we are employing a paradigm which is widely accepted and adhered to in diverse cultures and geographic regions around the world. Our responsibilities are both fiduciary and sacred.

That's true in spite of the more skeptical responses by some tradition-bound Western traders and market pundits, who either denigrate financial astrology as an intrinsically fraudulent analytical model, or who instead look for ways to co-opt astrological methodologies in the markets without fully exploring the empirical correlations that make modern financial astrology so valuable.

Even so, we have repeatedly found in our study of Bitcoin and other markets that the best approach to effective astro-trading is to integrate astrological analysis with technical analysis, with an understanding of key market fundamentals, and with time-tested tools for identifying market cycles and trend waves. We don't use planetary indicators in a vacuum, and in the practical world of putting real money at risk in the markets, we certainly don't try to trade solely on the basis of traditional astrological symbolism alone.

Within that framework, then, in this fourth approach to applying astrology to the markets we begin our analysis with cycle tools and technical indicators, and then see what kind of astrological factors provide confirmation for our conclusions.

In the case of Bitcoin, one of the most significant trading cycles seems to be 11.21 days. While this cycle in and of itself may not provide strong enough trading signals to be used in isolation as a sole timing indicator, its correlations with price swings in the cryptocurrency are nevertheless apparent enough to warrant our attention. So let's examine its implications a little more deeply.

Our earlier reference to the classic "day for a year" timing analogy may prove especially relevant here. It brings to mind the work of Carlos Garcia-Mata and Felix Shaffner, who published "Solar and Economic Relationships: A Preliminary Report" in the November 1934 issue of the *Quarterly Journal of Economics*.

These authors documented an 11.20-year rhythmic cycle in manufacturing productivity in the United States from 1875 through 1930, and postulated that it had a correlation with sunspot cycles. According to later research by Edward R. Dewey of the Foundation for the Study of Cycles, that 11.20-year business cycle continued to follow ideal behavior through 1953.

But the 11.21-day cycle in Bitcoin prices is more than just a microcosmic reflection of sunspot cycles. It is also connected to the orbital period of Venus.

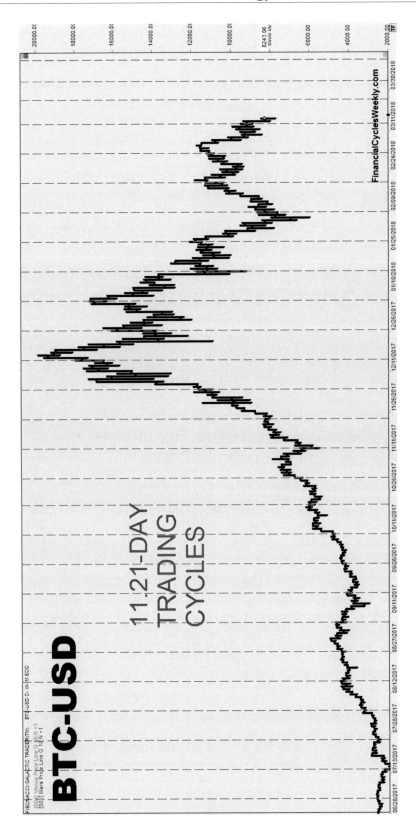

Venus takes 224.65 days to complete one passage around the Sun. When we look at the twentieth harmonic of that orbital period, 11.2325 days, we get a close approximation of the 11.21-day cycle evident in Bitcoin trading. In fact, the difference between these two intervals is only equivalent to about 32 minutes of clock time – not a bad degree of accuracy for an orbital process that takes nearly seven and a half months to complete!

Even though our conclusions are based on observations of the specific trading cycle that has been observed in Bitcoin, this correlation suggests that it can be helpful for us to take Venus cycles and relationships into consideration. Regardless of pre-existing biases for or against astrological methodologies, we'll definitely want to include Venus when we look at trading opportunities in Bitcoin, but with the full acknowledgment that Venus is not the sole determining factor in Bitcoin price fluctuations.

While this connection between an observed Bitcoin cycle and a planetary rhythm is certainly noteworthy, we need to keep in mind that we are looking at a specific harmonic division of the Venus cycle when we apply it in our Bitcoin forecasting and analysis. A twentieth-harmonic Venus cycle represents the motion of that planet through 18° in celestial longitude. But it can be somewhat challenging, if not completely impractical, to try to coordinate trading activity with precise degree positions in the motion of transiting planets.

A far more functional approach is to use instead the the tools for harmonic analysis that we described in our third approach to astro-trading, specifically the planetary price lines. Because we are looking at a cycle correlation with twentieth-harmonic Venus cycles, we can use twentieth-harmonic planetary price lines for Venus, even though they are not specifically coordinated with significant trading highs or lows for Bitcoin. While these planetary price lines obviously do not account for every price fluctuation in the Bitcoin trading, they do conform with a sufficient number of trading channels and significant points of support or resistance to give us a useful sense of the underlying trends and potential turning points in this market.

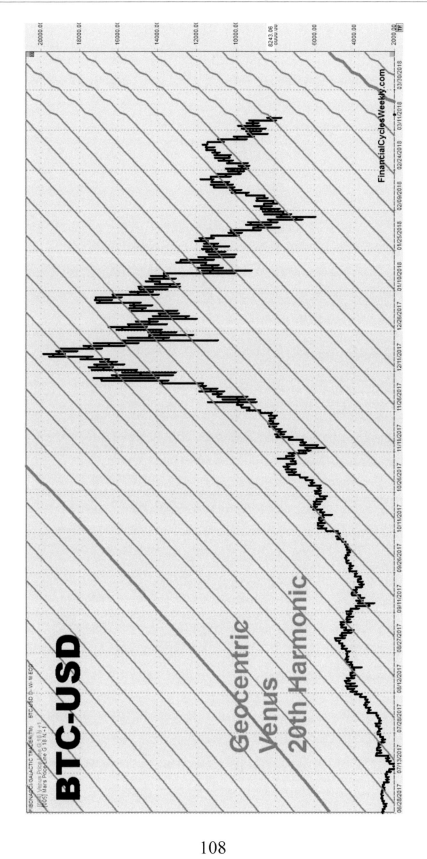

While the Bitcoin connection with Venus is certainly important, it is not the only planetary relationship that we have discovered in our research. There is also a verifiable Bitcoin trading cycle of 228 days.

This 228-day trading cycle coincides quite closely with a third-harmonic division of the orbital cycle of Mars. Mars completes its journey through the entire 360° of the zodiac in 686.93 days.

One-third of its orbital period is thus 228.97667 days, which is just 0.42% longer than the ideal Bitcoin trading cycle of 228 days.

And the Mars correspondences don't stop there.

There is an observed Bitcoin trading cycle of 114.5 days. This has an extremely close relationship with a sixth-harmonic division of the Mars orbital cycle, which is 114.48833 days. That means that the sixth-harmonic Mars cycle is shorter than the ideal Bitcoin cycle by just 1 minute and 41 seconds of clock time.

There are also observed Bitcoin trading cycles of 37.3 days and 39 days. These examples focus our attention on the eighteenth-harmonic division of the Mars orbital cycle, which is 38.16278 days.

There's obviously much to explore here, and Mars clearly has a strong connection to key cycles in Bitcoin trading.

For the present, however, we'll save a more in-depth investigation into the Mars cycle correlations with Bitcoin. Instead, let's add twentieth-harmonic planetary price lines for Mars to our trading chart that we have used to display the Venus planetary price line action. We're using the twentieth harmonic here just to coincide with our Venus price projections.

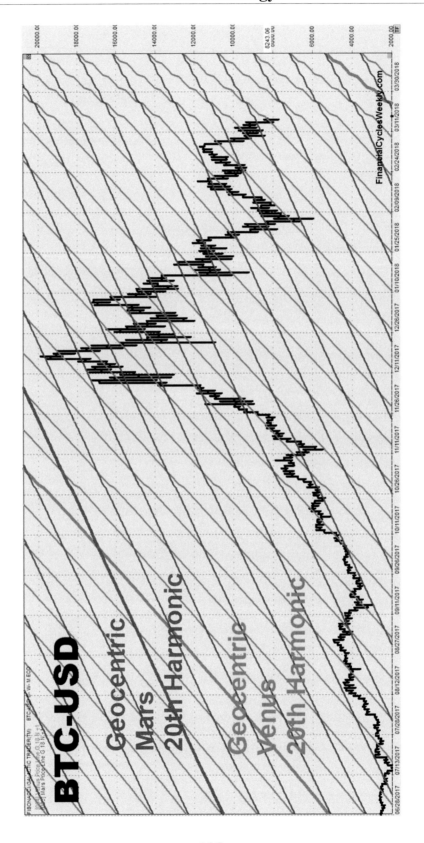

While the addition of the Mars price lines complicates our trading chart somewhat, it also provides us with additional insights. In many cases in which Bitcoin fails to conform precisely to Venus price action, it adheres to the Mars planetary price lines instead.

Although the interactions of Venus and Mars are hardly sufficient to give us reliable trading signals for Bitcoin by themselves, they do provide us with ample evidence of the key role that planetary phenomena play in the price action for this cryptocurrency. They also point the way toward other planetary alignments which may be profitably explored in our quest for mastery of Bitcoin trading cycles.

Based on our preliminary studies, it seems quite likely that the harmonics of Saturn and some of the transneptunian factors will ultimately prove to be significant. There are also significant correlations with transits of the Sun, which can give us useful seasonal indicators in Bitcoin trading.

Our investigations have shown that there are 20 periods of solar transit which have significant correlations to Bitcoin price action. They are evenly divided between bullish and bearish trends in Bitcoin.

We are reporting all of them here, grouped according to their net effects and listed in descending order of their impact and reliability. Keep in mind, however, that because we still have limited examples to use in our back-testing, these descriptions of the impact of solar phenomena are far from conclusive.

Even so, we believe that active Bitcoin traders will find them useful in investigating trading opportunities. In each case, the trading results that we describe are based on entering the trade when the transiting Sun is positioned at the first zodiac degree listed, and then exiting the trade when the Sun reaches the second zodiac degree.

Bullish Solar Transits For Bitcoin Trades

The Sun Transiting From 02° Taurus to 03° Gemini

Our back-testing for this solar transit was based on 6 previous examples.

The median gain for these trades was 3.6%. The mean gain was 100.8%.

This transit brought Bitcoin prices higher 100% of the time.

The Sun Transiting From 24° Libra to 24° Scorpio

Our back-testing for this solar transit was based on 6 previous examples.

The median gain for these trades was 22.5%. The mean gain was 65.3%.

This transit brought Bitcoin prices higher 100% of the time.

The Sun Transiting From 28° Aquarius to 29° Aries

Our back-testing for this solar transit was based on 7 previous examples.

The median gain for these trades was 21.6%. The mean gain was 63.0%.

This transit brought Bitcoin prices higher 85.7% of the time.

The Sun Transiting From 04° Gemini to 23° Gemini

Our back-testing for this solar transit was based on 7 previous examples.

The median gain for these trades was 8.7%. The mean gain was 27.2%.

This transit brought Bitcoin prices higher 85.7% of the time.

The Sun Transiting From 29° Scorpio to 04° Sagittarius

Our back-testing for this solar transit was based on 6 previous examples.

The median gain for these trades was 10.2%. The mean gain was 15.7%.

This transit brought Bitcoin prices higher 100% of the time.

The Sun Transiting From 15° Libra to 20° Libra

Our back-testing for this solar transit was based on 6 previous examples.

The median gain for these trades was 10.9%. The mean gain was 12.5%.

This transit brought Bitcoin prices higher 100% of the time.

The Sun Transiting From 28° Capricorn to 04° Aquarius

Our back-testing for this solar transit was based on 7 previous examples.

The median gain for these trades was 5.1%. The mean gain was 10.8%.

This transit brought Bitcoin prices higher 100% of the time.

The Sun Transiting From 04° Capricorn to 10° Capricorn

Our back-testing for this solar transit was based on 6 previous examples.

The median gain for these trades was 8.1%. The mean gain was 8.3%.

This transit brought Bitcoin prices higher 83.3% of the time.

The Sun Transiting From 15° Sagittarius to 20° Sagittarius

Our back-testing for this solar transit was based on 8 previous examples.

The median gain for these trades was 6.5%. The mean gain was 6.5%.

This transit brought Bitcoin prices higher 87.5% of the time.

The Sun Transiting From 05° Sagittarius to 10° Sagittarius

Our back-testing for this solar transit was based on 8 previous examples.

The median gain for these trades was 5.0%. The mean gain was 7.4%.

This transit brought Bitcoin prices higher 87.5% of the time.

Bearish Solar Transits For Bitcoin Trades

The Sun Transiting From 16° Capricorn to 25° Capricorn

Our back-testing for this solar transit was based on 8 previous examples.

The median loss for these trades was 10.7%. The mean loss was 7.5%.

This transit brought Bitcoin prices lower 75% of the time.

The Sun Transiting From 27° Gemini to 03° Cancer

Our back-testing for this solar transit was based on 5 previous examples.

The median loss for these trades was 3.7%. The mean loss was 5.4%.

This transit brought Bitcoin prices lower 100% of the time.

The Sun Transiting From 19° Virgo to 28° Virgo

Our back-testing for this solar transit was based on 8 previous examples.

The median loss for these trades was 5.4%. The mean loss was 4.9%.

This transit brought Bitcoin prices lower 87.5% of the time.

The Sun Transiting From 08° Libra to 13° Libra

Our back-testing for this solar transit was based on 6 previous examples.

The median loss for these trades was 4.8%. The mean loss was 4.3%.

This transit brought Bitcoin prices lower 75% of the time.

The Sun Transiting From 23° Leo to 00° Virgo

Our back-testing for this solar transit was based on 6 previous examples.

The median loss for these trades was 1.6%. The mean loss was 5.8%.

This transit brought Bitcoin prices lower 83.3% of the time.

The Sun Transiting From 16° Aquarius to 21° Aquarius

Our back-testing for this solar transit was based on 8 previous examples.

The median loss for these trades was 2.9%. The mean loss was 5.2%.

This transit brought Bitcoin prices lower 75% of the time.

The Sun Transiting From 08° Cancer to 17° Cancer

Our back-testing for this solar transit was based on 7 previous examples.

The median loss for these trades was 5.5%. The mean loss was 2.1%.

This transit brought Bitcoin prices lower 71.4% of the time.

The Sun Transiting From 04° Virgo to 11° Virgo

Our back-testing for this solar transit was based on 7 previous examples.

The median loss for these trades was 4.7%. The mean loss was 1.5%.

This transit brought Bitcoin prices lower 71.4% of the time.

The Sun Transiting From 20° Cancer to 26° Cancer

Our back-testing for this solar transit was based on 6 previous examples.

The median loss for these trades was 1.4%. The mean loss was 1.2%.

This transit brought Bitcoin prices lower 83.3% of the time.

The Sun Transiting From 08° Leo to 18° Leo

Our back-testing for this solar transit was based on 8 previous examples.

The median loss for these trades was 2.3%.

But there was a mean *gain* for these trades of 0.7%.

This transit brought Bitcoin prices lower 75% of the time.

While our understanding of the nuances of Bitcoin astrology is still very much in its infancy, through this cycle-based methodology we have already begun to detect some potential correspondences between planetary alignments and significant price movements in the cryptocurrency. While they seem to have great promise, we are presenting them here primarily as suggestions for future research and for trading verification, in the hope that other financial astrologers will share their insights and observations to contribute to a combined effort that continues to advance Bitcoin astrology.

Please remember, however, that these preliminary efforts at defining Bitcoin trading cycles are far from conclusive. While our back-testing has thus far shown a high level of correlation and a strong probability of cycles continuing to repeat, in all cases our conclusions are based on a relatively small number of trading iterations, and the data may or may not be statistically significant. With that in mind, we want to underscore the fact that it's best to view these planetary correlations as hypotheses for further research, rather than as proven strategies that can give us slam-dunk trading opportunities.

With those disclaimers and caveats in mind, our research has revealed the following transit-to-transit planetary alignments, all derived from observations of Bitcoin trading cycles, which seem to have special significance in Bitcoin trading activity. We've listed two examples that connect with Bitcoin trading tops, and two that connect with Bitcoin trading bottoms. In each case, there is one higher-frequency cycle and one slower-moving cycle represented.

Aspects for Bitcoin Trading Tops

Mars/Cupido Waning Square

This alignment has coincided with Bitcoin trading tops 80% of the times that it has occurred. The best trading strategy to use with this aspect is to sell Bitcoin short 4 days after the date of the aspect, and then buy to cover the position 9 days after the aspect.

The next times that this aspect will occur are October 2, 2019; September 17, 2021; September 3, 2023; August 19, 2025; August 2, 2027; July 9, 2029; December 19, 2030; and November 27, 2032.

Jupiter/Poseidon Waning Trine

Because of the slower planetary motion involved, this aspect is much less frequent, but it still sets up powerful trading opportunities. It has corresponded with Bitcoin trading tops 100% of the time during its previous iterations. The best short-term trading strategy is to sell Bitcoin short 2 days before the exact Jupiter/Poseidon alignment, and then buy to cover 2 days after the exact aspect.

The next times this aspect will occur are August 20, 2025; February 1, 2026; and April 14, 2026.

Aspects for Bitcoin Trading Bottoms

Venus/Admetos Waning Trine

This alignment has coincided with Bitcoin trading bottoms 75% of the time during its previous iterations. It seems to have a very strong connection with Bitcoin as a trigger for bullish trading action.

The best strategy for trading this alignment is to buy Bitcoin on the date that the aspect occurs, and then sell 24 days later.

The next times this aspect will occur are March 1, 2019; December 20, 2019; February 2, 2021; March 8, 2022; and January 4, 2023.

Jupiter/Kronos Waning Sextile

This is another infrequent configuration, but it has previously been associated with a strong gain in a short period of time. The optimum trading strategy is to buy Bitcoin 1 day before the exact aspect, and then sell 20 days after the aspect occurs.

This planetary alignment will take place next on August 19, 2023; September 14, 2023; and March 16, 2024.

5. Midpoints and Planetary Pictures

As financial astrologers, however, we don't stop with the determination of market-derived cycles alone. Once we have found a probable trading cycle based on market back-testing, and have had an opportunity to examine that cycle in the light of traditional astrology and harmonic analysis, we can add even more refinement and depth of understanding if we employ the unique perspective of symmetrical astrology. Looking for correlations, we can often open up a richer and more intuitive appreciation of the underlying cycles in the market, and then move into research that is even more solidly based in astrology to further refine our forecasts and trading expectations.

The examination of horoscope midpoints is a tool that offers us particularly useful opportunities for refining our analysis of any horoscope, but it is surprisingly underused by many astrologers. When we examine midpoint structures in financial horoscopes, we can gain deeper insights into the underlying forces at work in market dynamics. We can also open up the possibility of identifying additional trading opportunities with remarkable precision.

Midpoints were used extensively in the Arabic astrology of previous centuries; their application was revived by the German astrologer Reinhold Ebertin in his approach to Cosmobiology, and by Alfred Witte and his students in the Hamburg School of Uranian astrology. The Germans referred to midpoints as "half-sums", which provides some useful insights into their mathematical determination in the horoscope. The term also reinforces the thinking in the current presentation of midpoints in Symmetrical astrology, under the intellectual leadership of Gary Christen.

Some midpoint structures are simply representations of what traditional astrology considers planetary aspects. But there are many dynamic angular relationships between planets that have demonstrable power in impacting events, and a considerable number of them do not fall into boundaries defined by the aspects of traditional astrology. As John Addey, the great advocate of harmonic astrology, observed, "in the Ebertin system. . . only multiples of 45° are thought to be valid aspects for midpoints; however, I doubt that the last word has been said."

Addey made that comment in 1976. Now, more than 40 years later, the last word has still not been said. And the study of midpoints is an important key to unlocking the incredible potential hidden in the horoscope.

By far the most useful tool for discovering and delineating midpoint structures is the 90° dial. As a physical device, it allows us to move a pointer to any degree position on a transparent overlay of the horoscope. On the dial, the 360° of the zodiac have essentially been folded over themselves twice and then projected onto a circle representing a 90° span. Thanks to the brilliant work of Gary Christen at Astrolabe, the physical dial has been captured in a precise way in the Nova Chartwheels software program. The software allows the user to employ a movable pointer on the computer screen, highlighting midpoint structures and providing additional information in real time.

As an example of the ways in which an awareness of midpoints can expand our awareness of horoscope dimensions, let's take another look at the chart for the historic Bitcoin trading high on December 17, 2017. Here is the traditional horoscope wheel for that event:

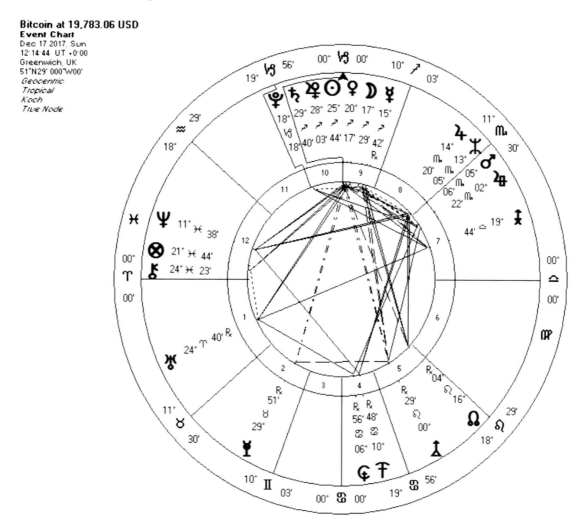

As we have noted before, Mars carries a lot of weight in this horoscope, but the chart is primarily dominated by the Grand Trine pattern and by the extraordinary alignment of the chart angles with the cardinal points. When we put the same horoscope onto the 90° dial, we have chosen to align the movable pointer with the position of Mars, with reference to its key role in the conventional horoscope. And that's where the dial's power becomes evident.

Bitcoin at 19,783.06 USD
Greenwich, UK
Dec 17 2017
12:14:44 PM UT

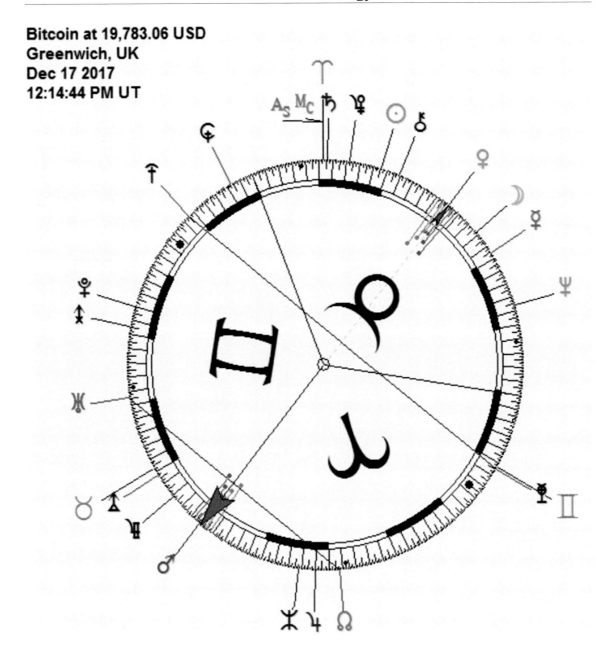

By aligning the pointer with Mars, we at once see its activation of Venus, which is at the smaller pointer on the opposite side of the dial. This is an eighth-harmonic alignment, indicating the semi-square between the two planets. But what's interesting here is the activation of two midpoint structures as well – Uranus and the True Lunar Node; and the midpoint of Kronos and Admetos. Note that there aren't Ptolemaic aspects between either of these planetary pairs evident in the traditional horoscope wheel, so their connections are uniquely revealed in the presentation on the 90° dial.

The Node/Uranus midpoint is indicative of sudden events, unexpected connections, and exciting action. That's certainly descriptive of the trading environment when Bitcoin hit it record high.

The midpoint of the two transneptunian factors Kronos and Admetos is equally apropos. It describes odd individuals or entities (like Bitcoin itself), as well as "differences in altitude". It's specifically linked to hills or mountains (including, no doubt, market peaks), and to the fall of a leader or a descent from a high place. So it's definitely descriptive of a record-breaking trading top.

While these midpoints themselves add strong significant to our understanding of the horoscope, when we factor in the presence of Mars, we add an extra dimension. Mars, as a third element, converts a simple midpoint structure to a planetary picture – a combination of the energies of three or more planets in a dynamic and highly influential relationship.

The presence of Mars in the planetary pictures with Node/Uranus and Kronos/Admetos adds extra dynamism, bringing a highly active and even confrontational or belligerent attitude to the mix. In this light, it's worth noting that the Bitcoin trading high was an event that wasn't universally celebrated. In fact, the mere notion that Bitcoin had reached such an absurdly high price level brought out some open animosity in some quarters.

Planetary pictures can be particularly useful when we are looking at configurations that move fairly rapidly. For example, in buying Bitcoin at 8,081.64 on February 11, 2018, we unwittingly entered a trade with a surprisingly powerful success trigger – the transiting Moon. At the time of the trade, it created a planetary picture with the Venus/Jupiter midpoint – a classic "good luck" signature. And the trade brought good luck indeed. Closing the position at 11,256.43 on February 20 returned a profit of 39.2% in just 9 days.

Bitcoin Trade Setup
New York, NY
Feb 11 2018
9:25:00 PM EST

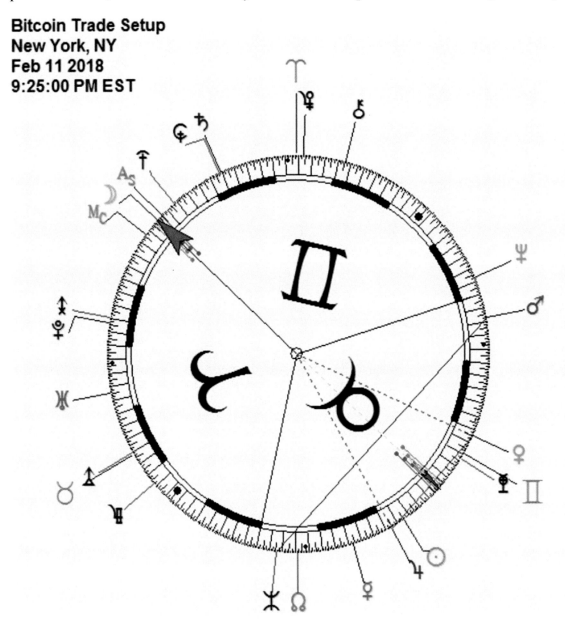

While we're free to apply any of these approaches to Bitcoin trading, the best approach is typically to use them all. With multiple confirmations of our analysis, we are far more likely to have the confidence to take a trade – and that's when we have an opportunity to make money in the markets!

Bitcoin Horoscopes

Tim Bost

As we move forward with advancing Bitcoin astrology, it's essential for us to have accurate horoscopes to work with. In compiling horoscope data relevant to the history of bitcoin, we've been careful to determine the times and locations of events as precisely as possible. When a time of day is unknown, we have set the horoscope charts for noon.

For astrologers, the concepts of time and location are synergistically interwoven in a way that defines the unique essence of a horoscope: a representation of a specific instant in time, as experienced at a specific location.

This synergy was most directly experienced prior to the closing years of the Nineteenth Century, when the advent of the railroads gave birth to the concept and creation of standardized time zones.

In those days, and for many previous centuries, time itself was defined by location. You could estimate the time of day by the shadow on the face of a sundial, or you could go to the village square and consult the clock on the church steeple or on the courthouse tower.

That public display of a clock essentially tied time to a specific location. If the clock was efficiently maintained and performed as it should ("like clockwork"), it showed local mean time accurately.

But local mean time was accurate only in a particular location; if you went to a village fifty miles away, you'd see a different time shown on the tower in that town square.

An accurate clock on public display showed the "official" time for the town. If you were fortunate enough to own a pocket watch, you could walk into town and set your watch to synchronize with that public clock.

Then, later in the day, if someone asked you "Do you have the time?", you could take out your trusted timepiece and provide a precise answer. You indeed literally "had the time" – in fact, you had gone to town, picked it up, and carried it home with you!

That reliance on official time from a specific location depended, of course, on clocks that functioned properly. The craft of clock making and clock repair was highly valued as a truly honorable profession. But in most cases, knowing the time was a matter of accepted norms rather than scientific precision.

In that light, there was as much genuine grievance as there was wry Irish humor in the references that the residents of Cork, Ireland made about the steeple on St. Anne Shandon's Church, which displayed four clocks facing the cardinal points of the compass. The locals called it the "Four-Faced Liar" – none of the four clocks ever agreed with the other three!

Timing and Locating Events in a Distributed Network

In the age of the internet, however, our experience of time and space has changed quite dramatically. In the United Kingdom school officials have begun removing analog clocks from classrooms because the students no longer know how to tell time on a circular dial. Time has gone digital, and clock repair is now a dying craft.

This new experience of time is an integral part of the internet environment. Online transactions and forum postings are often timed to the precise second. But while computer servers do have specific locations, cyberspace itself is inherently omnipresent. Time has become divorced from location.

In fact, it is that omnipresence itself that gives the blockchain its power to verify transactions. Satoshi Nakamoto's Bitcoin whitepaper was significant because it provided the first truly workable protocol for recording and verifying financial transactions in a distributed network,

The Bitcoin blockchain records its transactions as timestamps in a format known as Unix time or Epoch time, which is sometimes also referred to as POSIX time. It represents the total number of seconds in clock time that have elapsed since 00:00:00 UTC on January 1, 1970. This time notation does not change in different locations, making it useful for blockchain applications and other internet transactions as well, which typically involve simultaneous events in multiple locations.

Based on that precedent of a UTC reference point, we have chosen to erect horoscopes for non-location-specific online events (like transactions on a distributed network) for Greenwich in the United Kingdom, at the latitude of the observatory which marks the longitudinal Prime Meridian, the origin point for the various time zones in the world. Because of the somewhat synthetic nature of these "global" horoscopes, we prefer not to put too much emphasis on house placements and planetary house rulerships when interpreting those charts.

When, however, there is specific documentation of an online event having originated at a particular location, or when a particular location is significantly impacted by an otherwise non-local event, we use that location in our horoscope calculations, along with the Unix timestamp converted to UTC. In such cases we are typically a bit more confident in considering the horoscope houses in our assessment of astrological potential.

In this collection of Bitcoin horoscopes we've included some horoscopes for events which long pre-dated the advent of Bitcoin itself. We believe that these precursor charts are worth contemplating in our efforts to understand the full social and economic effects of Bitcoin, and they may also prove useful in some way as we refine our analysis and continue to look for more effective Bitcoin trading strategies.

At the other end of the spectrum, we've not included any horoscopes for other cryptocurrencies in this collection. While it's certain that many of them will become important in future years, the sheer number of these new tokens and their relatively short trading histories has led us to the conclusion that they will best be dealt with in future volumes. So our focus here is exclusively on the most important events we have been able to document in the history of Bitcoin.

Some of the horoscopes presented here reflect technological breakthroughs and innovations, or document events within the blockchain itself. Others involve criminal activities, court cases, or regulatory rulings. Some are public events or media activities which reflect changing trends in the public awareness of Bitcoin. In every case, however, we think they are worth examining in an effort to get a complete understanding of Bitcoin and its future.

Dollar-Gold Redemption Stopped

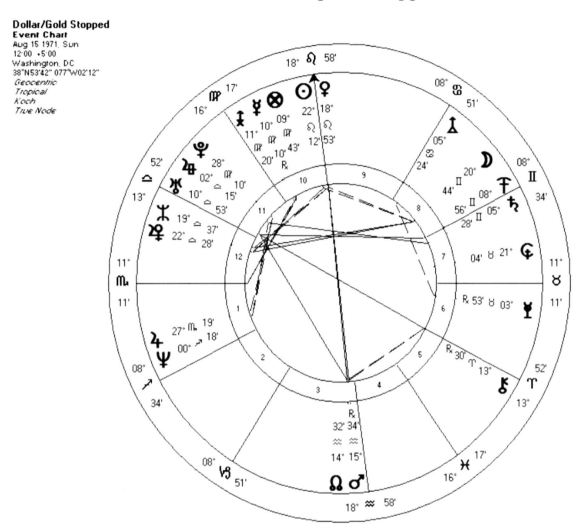

Dollar/Gold Stopped
Event Chart
Aug 15 1971, Sun
12:00 +5:00
Washington, DC
38°N53'42" 077°W02'12"
Geocentric
Tropical
Koch
True Node

U.S. President Richard M. Nixon announced that the dollar would no longer be redeemable in gold, effectively ending the international monetary protocols established by the Bretton Woods Agreement. The move allowed the dollar to float, opening the door for the possibility of currency trading and ultimately, for speculation in cryptocurrencies as well.

David Chaum Demonstrates DigiCash

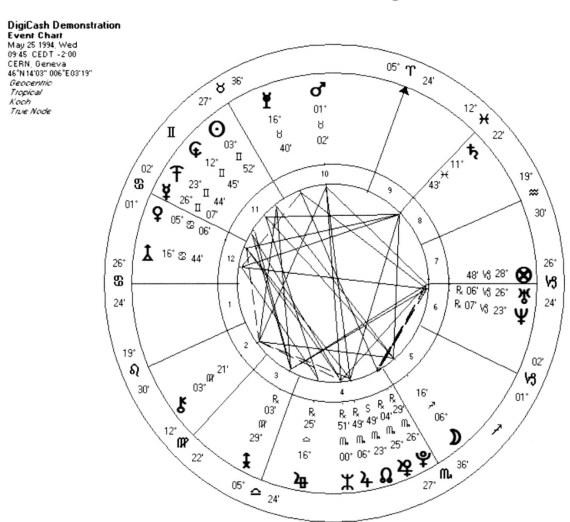

DigiCash Demonstration
Event Chart
May 25 1994, Wed
09:45 CEDT -2:00
CERN, Geneva
46°N14'03" 006°E03'19"
Geocentric
Tropical
Koch
True Node

Bitcoin was not the first attempt to establish protocols for the electronic transfer of money on a peer-to-peer basis. An important precursor was the work done on DigiCash by David Chaum, an American computer programmer and cryptographic pioneer who also developed the concept behind ecash, an electronic transfer system designed to preserve the anonymity of users.

On May 27, 1994 Dr. David Chaum, the Managing Director of Digi-Cash, put out a press release announcing that "Payment from any personal computer to any other workstation, over email or Internet, has been demonstrated for the first time, using electronic cash technology."

Chaum had actually demonstrated the product two days earlier, during his keynote address on "Effective Rules In Cyberspace" at the First Conference on the World Wide Web, which was held at the CERN laboratories for the European Organization for Nuclear Research near Geneva, Switzerland.

"Electronic cash has the privacy of paper cash," Chaum noted during his presentation at the conference, "while achieving the high security required for electronic network environments exclusively through innovations in public key cryptography."

The plenary session of the First Conference on the World Wide Web began at 9:30 a.m on Wednesday, May 25 with welcoming remarks from CERN Director of Research Walter Hoogland. Chaum's presentation was next on the programme of events.

David Chaum originally described the underlying conceptual framework for the "blind signature" technology behind DigiCash in an article on "Achieving Electronic Privacy" in the August, 1992 issue of ***Scientific American***.

Introduction of Hashcash

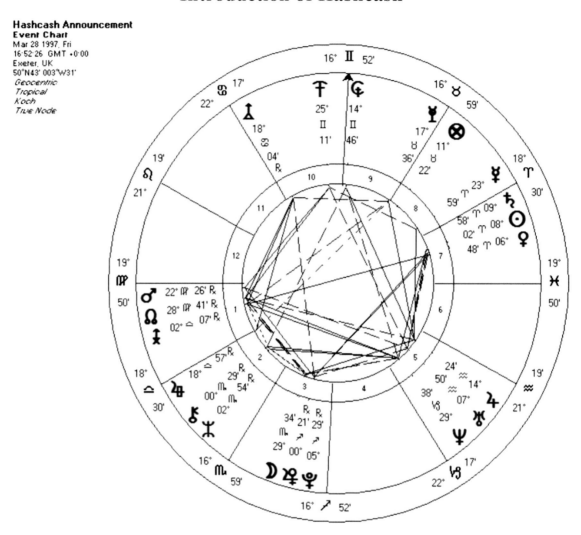

Adam Back, a British cryptographer focusing on anti-spam technologies, invented a proof-of-work system called Hashcash. It was an important precursor to the proof-of-work protocols in the Bitcoin blockchain.

Registration of Bitcoin.org Domain Name

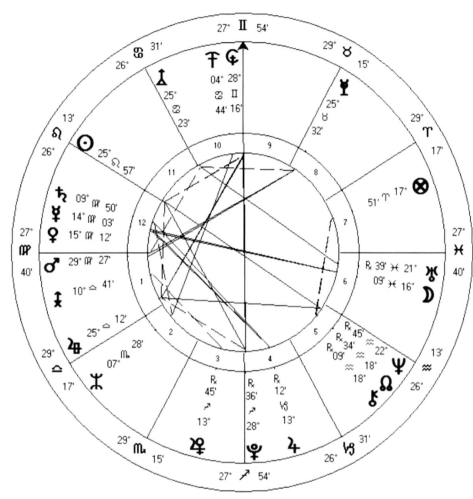

The first recorded appearance of the name Bitcoin came with the registration of an internet domain name, bitcoin.org. The registration document was filed in Panama, with the name of the registrant kept confidential.

Lehman Brothers Bankruptcy Decision

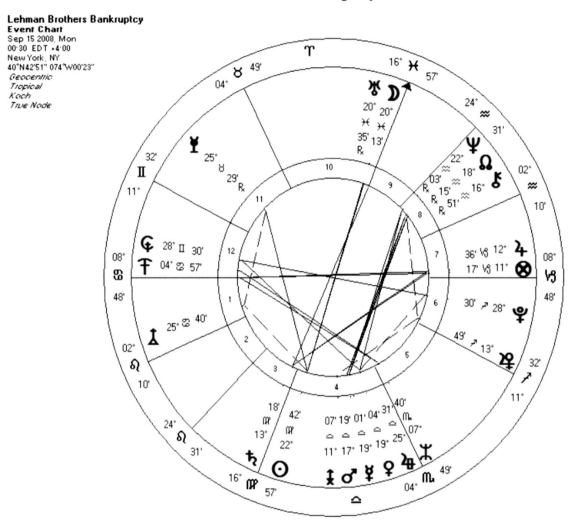

Lehman Brothers Bankruptcy
Event Chart
Sep 15 2008, Mon
00:30 EDT +4:00
New York, NY
40°N42'51" 074°W00'23"
Geocentric
Tropical
Koch
True Node

The decision that Lehman Brothers was going to file for bankruptcy in the midst of a metastasizing financial meltdown was in many ways the event that was most emblematic of the global financial meltdown of 2008. As an event with a massive psychological impact, it helped set the stage for the introduction of the Bitcoin concept six weeks later.

Bitcoin Proposal Whitepaper Published

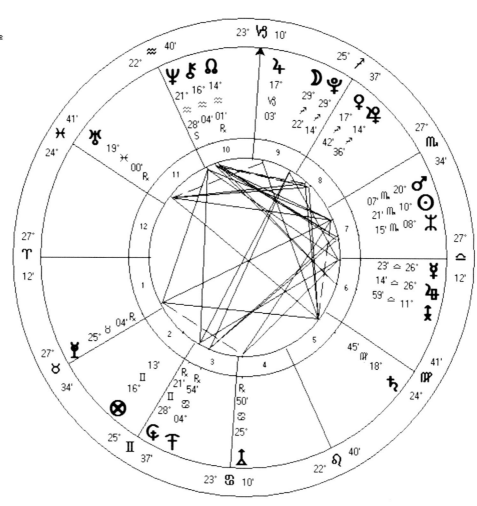

Bitcoin Proposal
Event Chart
Nov 2 2008, Sun
17:56:27 AWST -8:00
Singapore, Singapore
01°N17' 103°E51'
Geocentric
Tropical
Koch
True Node

Although the description of Bitcoin by Satoshi Nakamoto was dated October 31, 2008, its first recorded publication was on a chat forum a couple of days later. This is an essential horoscope for understanding the huge potential impact of Bitcoin on economic and social structures.

Genesis Block – Sydney

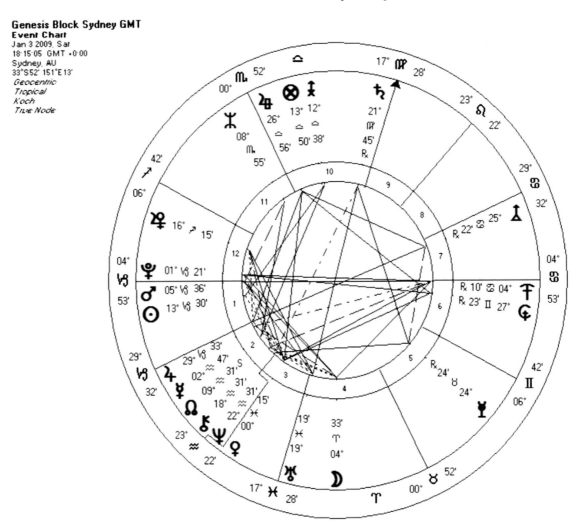

Genesis Block Sydney GMT
Event Chart
Jan 3 2009, Sat
18:15:05 GMT +0:00
Sydney, AU
33°S52' 151°E13'
Geocentric
Tropical
Koch
True Node

The initial Bitcoin transaction, recorded as the first or Genesis Block on the Bitcoin blockchain, signaled the move from a concept to an active network. The block had this text embedded: "The Times 03/Jan/2009 Chancellor on brink of second bailout for banks." – an authenticating time stamp, but also a derisive comment on the upheaval and instability in the traditional banking system. Satoshi Nakamoto mined the first block as a non-local event. The Genesis Block is represented by several different horoscopes set for varying locations, which are favored by various astrologers. We're sharing three of them here. In this chart for Sydney, note the use of GMT.

Genesis Block – Tokyo

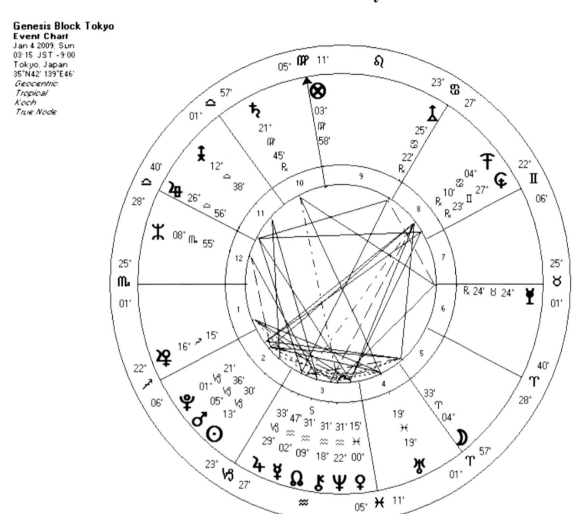

The Genesis Block horoscope set for Tokyo, Japan not only features different degree positions for the chart angles and for the Part of Fortune – it also shows the event occurring on a different date than the Sydney chart. Note, however, that the planetary positions (including the all-important position of the Moon) reveal that only the location has changed here; it's a horoscope for the same moment as the Sydney Genesis Block chart.

Genesis Block – Greenwich

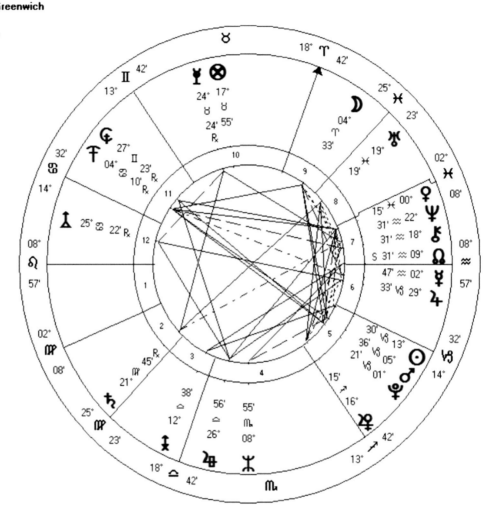

In keeping with our decision to use Greenwich positional coordinates and UTC time notation for non-location-specific events that take place on the internet, we've added this Genesis Block horoscope. In comparing the three versions of this horoscope, pay particular attention to the most angular planets: Mars and Kronos in the Sydney horoscope, Admetos in the Tokyo horoscope, and the True North Lunar Node in this Greenwich horoscope. They all have significant symbolic connections with different aspects of Bitcoin, so the choice of one of these charts in preference to the others may imply subtle connotations revealing biases or attitudes about Bitcoin and its ultimate future.

New Liberty Standard

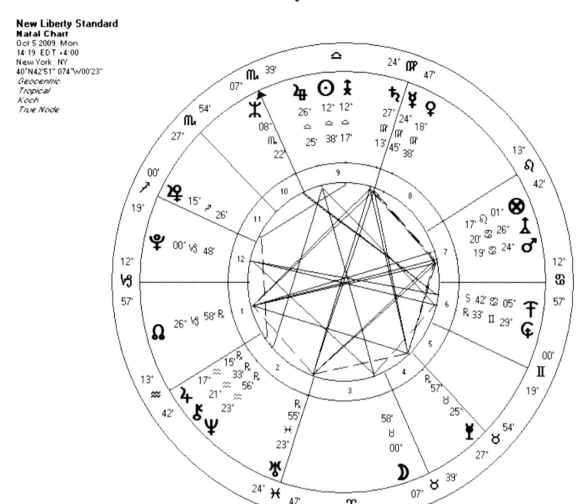

New Liberty Standard
Natal Chart
Oct 5 2009, Mon
14:19 EDT +4:00
New York, NY
40°N42'51" 074°W00'23"
Geocentric
Tropical
Koch
True Node

New Liberty Standard opens a service to buy and sell bitcoin, with an initial exchange rate of 1,309.03 BTC to one U.S. dollar, or about eight-hundredths of a cent per Bitcoin. This was the first publication of an exchange rate for Bitcoin. The exchange rate is derived from the cost of the electricity used by a computer to generate, a block in the blockchain, or "mine" the currency.

First Bitcoin Exchange For Fiat Currency

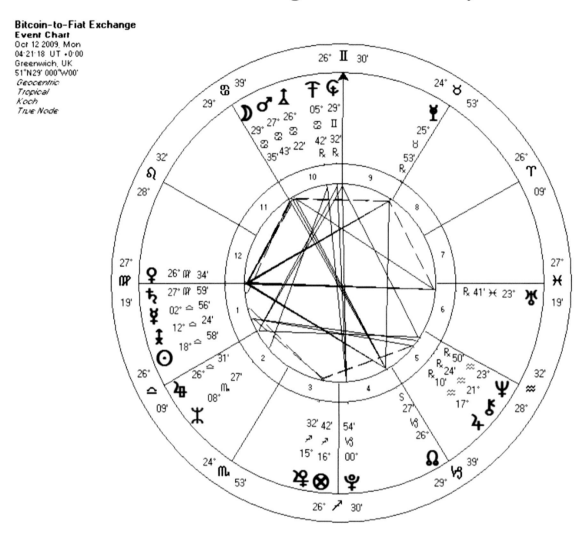

Using PayPal to complete the transaction, New Liberty Standard bought 5,050 Bitcoin from Sirius (Martti Malmi) for $5.02, equating to roughly one tenth of a cent per Bitcoin. This was the first known exchange of Bitcoin for any fiat currency, in the case U.S. dollars.

142

Bitcoin Pizza Purchase

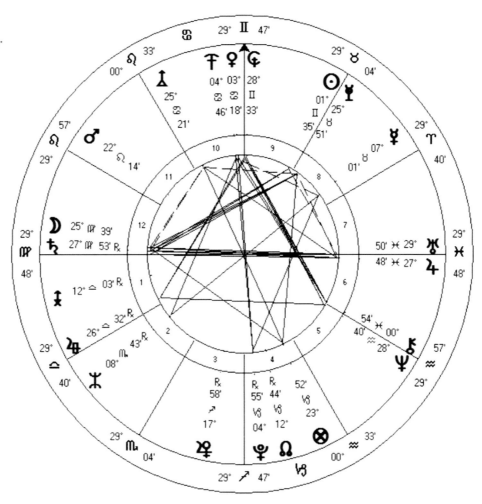

BitcoinTalk chat forum participant laszlo (Laszlo Hanyecz) paid 10,000 BTC for two pizzas delivered to his house in Jacksonville, Florida. The two pizzas were valued at about $25, and were ordered and paid for by another BitcoinTalk user, jercos. After looking in the forum for several days for someone to take him up on the idea of the purchase, laszlo posted the message that "I just wanted to report that I successfully traded 10,000 bitcoins for pizza." This first-ever Bitcoin payment for a physical item assigned the first concrete valuation to Bitcoin – about $0.0025 per coin.

Bitcoin Described In Slashdot Post

Bitcoin Post On Slashdot
Event Chart
Jul 11 2010, Sun
17:09 UT +0:00
Greenwich, UK
51°N29' 000°W00'
Geocentric
Tropical
Koch
True Node

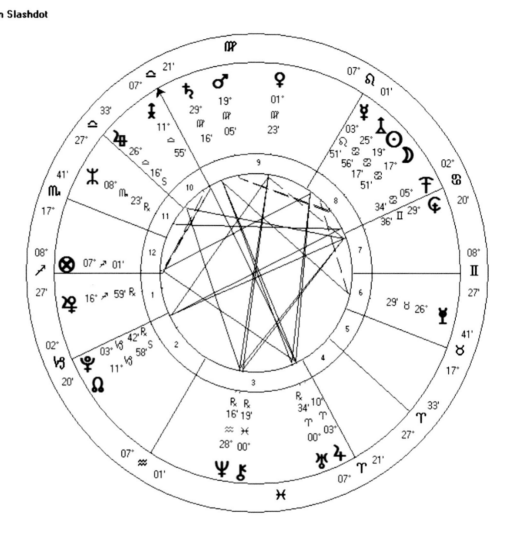

The release of Bitcoin version 0.3 was featured in a discussion forum on slashdot.org, a popular news and technology website. "How's this for a disruptive technology?" the post asked. "Bitcoin is a peer-to-peer, network-based digital currency with no central bank, and no transaction fees." It added that "The community is hopeful the currency will remain outside the reach of any government." Reaching a large audience of technophiles, the post brought many new enthusiasts on board, driving the exchange value of a single Bitcoin up nearly tenfold, from approximately $0.008 to $0.08 in just five days.

Mt. Gox Bitcoin Exchange

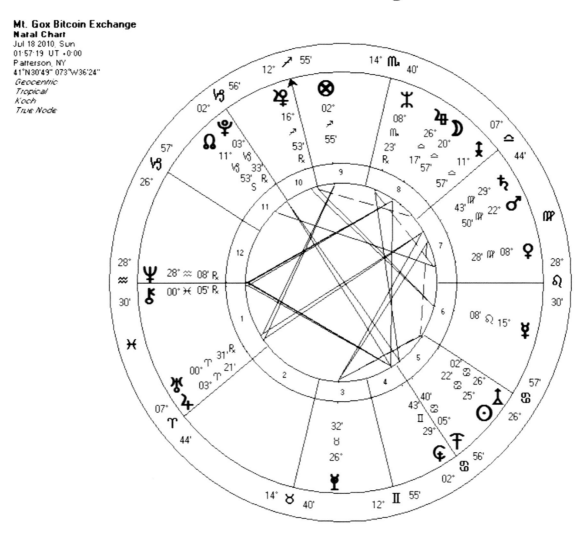

Jed McCaleb, an American programmer best known for creating the successful eDonkey peer-to-peer network in 2000, announced the launch of Mt. Gox, a new full-time Bitcoin exchange. The functionality of the exchange was based on a prior, abandoned project of McCaleb's in which he had tried to create an online exchange for Magic: The Gathering gaming cards. Mt. Gox would grow to become the dominant force in Bitcoin trading for several years.

Strange Block 74638

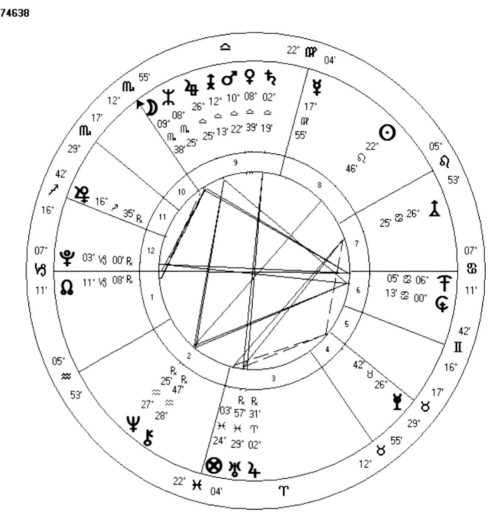

A terse post on BitcoinTalk by Satoshi Nakamoto spread the alarm: "*** WARNING *** We are investigating a problem. DO NOT TRUST ANY TRANSACTIONS THAT HAPPENED AFTER 15.08.2010 17:05 UTC (block 74638) until the issue is resolved."

A fraudulent transaction had generated 184,467,440,737.08554078 Bitcoins – nearly 9,000 times as many as can legitimately exist in the entire system. The oddity was quickly spotted by the Bitcoin community, and a fixed version of the Bitcoin software was released within hours. By the next day, the "hard fork" corrected blockchain overtook the exploited one, and Bitcoin was back to normal – but not before the market had been badly shaken.

Strange Block 74638
Greenwich, UK
Aug 15 2010
5:05:57 PM UT

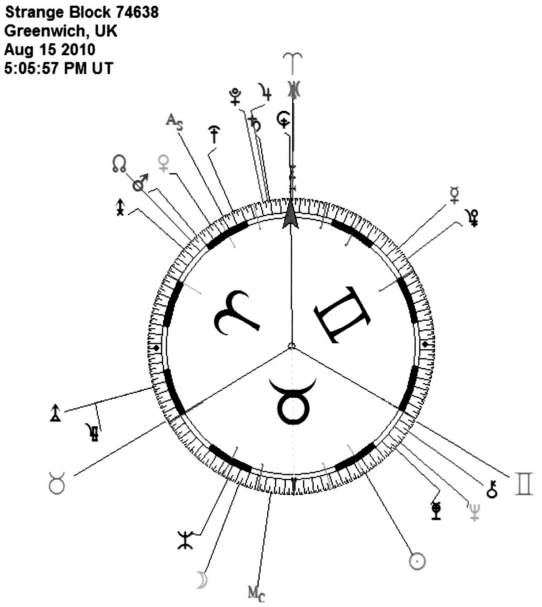

Particularly striking in this horoscope is the Aries point activation of the planetary picture Zeus + Vulcanus – Poseidon. It signals "Impressive proofs; foolproof evidence. Good and reliable tests. Mighty mental creation. Great mental efforts. Happiness about the correctness of one's reasoning."

Sale of the Mt. Gox Exchange

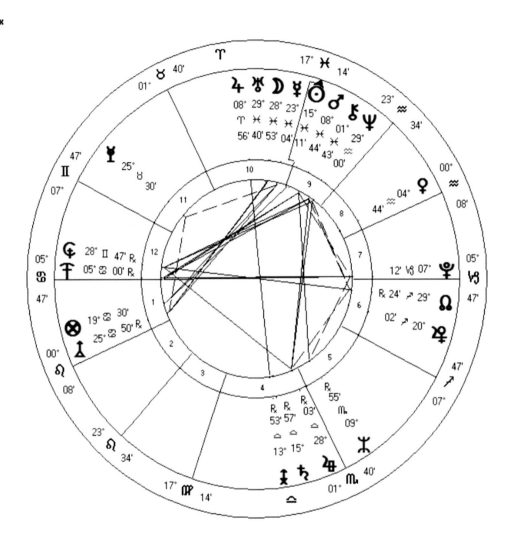

Sale of Mt. Gox
Event Chart
Mar 6 2011, Sun
12:00 JST -9:00
Tokyo, Japan
35°N42' 139°E46'
Geocentric
Tropical
Koch
True Node

Just nine months after it opened, the Mt. Gox Exchange had become an overwhelming success. Founder Jed McCaleb, who was struggling to keep up with the escalating demands of the business, sold mtgox.com to Mark Karpelès of Tibanne Ltd.

Gawker Publishes Silk Road Article

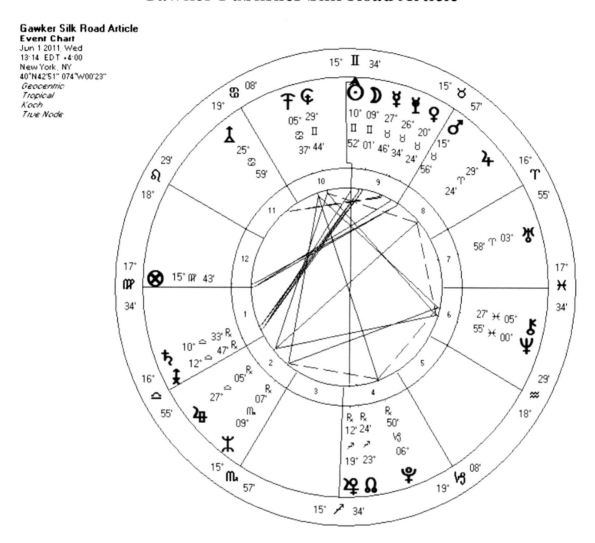

Gawker Silk Road Article
Event Chart
Jun 1 2011, Wed
13:14 EDT +4:00
New York, NY
40°N42'51" 074°W00'23"
Geocentric
Tropical
Koch
True Node

When the online publication Gawker.com released an article by Adrian Chen titled "The Underground Website Where You Can Buy Any Drug Imaginable" it didn't take long for it to go viral. The article described the Silk Road website as being like "Amazon – if Amazon sold mind-altering chemicals." Chen reported that "As for transactions, Silk Road doesn't accept credit cards, PayPal, or any other form of payment that can be traced or blocked." All purchases had to be paid for in Bitcoin, "the online equivalent of a brown paper bag of cash." The article triggered an enormous surge of interest in Bitcoin.

Mt. Gox Hacked

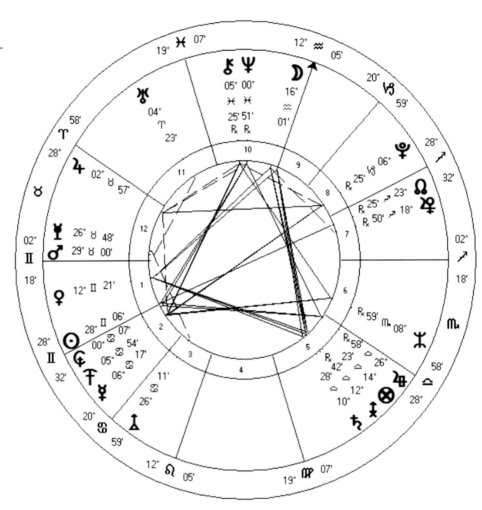

Hackers downloaded a copy of the Mt. Gox user database, including email addresses and insecure passwords. Using new-found administrator-level access, they placed countless offers to sell nonexistent Bitcoins, falsely deflating prices until they dropped to just $0.01 per coin. Mt. Gox reverses the fraudulent transactions and halts trading for seven days, and two other large exchanges issue temporary halts while reviewing their own security. A leaked copy of the database was then used to launch attacks against MyBitcoin online wallet accounts, stealing over 4,019 Bitcoin from roughly 600 wallets.

CBS Announces "The Good Wife" Bitcoin Episode

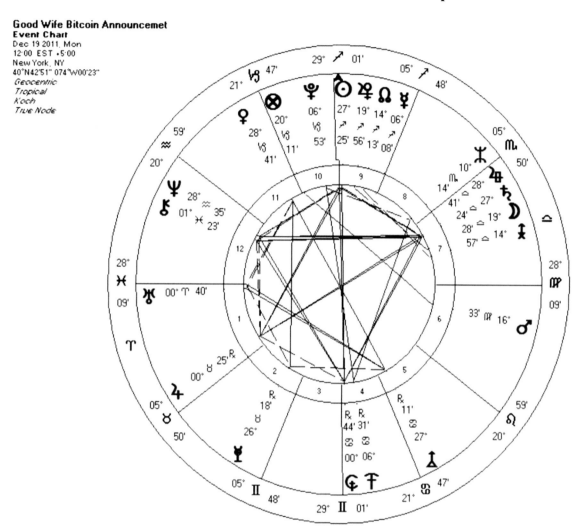

An announcement from CBS Television confirmed rumors that the network was about to release an episode of its popular dramatic series "The Good Wife" focusing on Bitcoin. Industry gossip about the program had been discussed on Bitcoin chat forums since November 29. After the initial announcement of this upcoming episode, investors bet big on the show to catapult prices to new highs, driving the price of Bitcoin from $3.41 on December 19 to $4.22 ten days later.

"Bitcoin For Dummies" Airs on "The Good Wife"

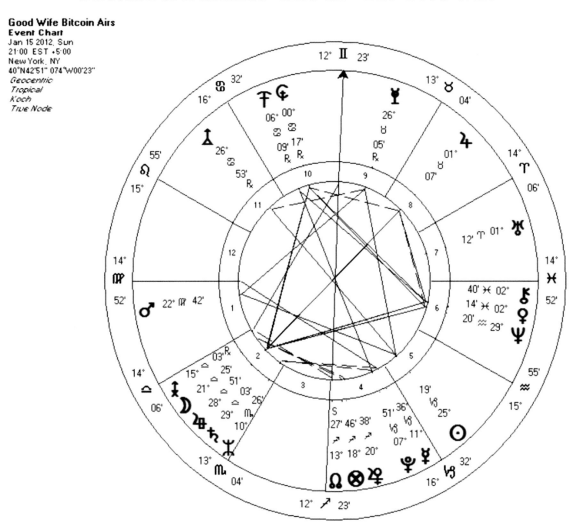

About 9.45 million viewers tuned in to watch "Bitcoin for Dummies" on CBS. In the episode Alicia Florick and Lockhart/Gardner face off against the U.S. Treasury Department and aid Dylan Stack, a lawyer representing the creator of Bitcoin – a mysterious online currency. Stack is pressured to reveal the name of the anonymous Bitcoin creator so the government can prosecute him for creating a currency in direct competition with the US dollar. But the Treasury Department changes tactics and decides to prosecute Stack himself as the Bitcoin creator. Bitcoin prices were stagnant after the show's airing.

Web Host Linode Confirms Hack

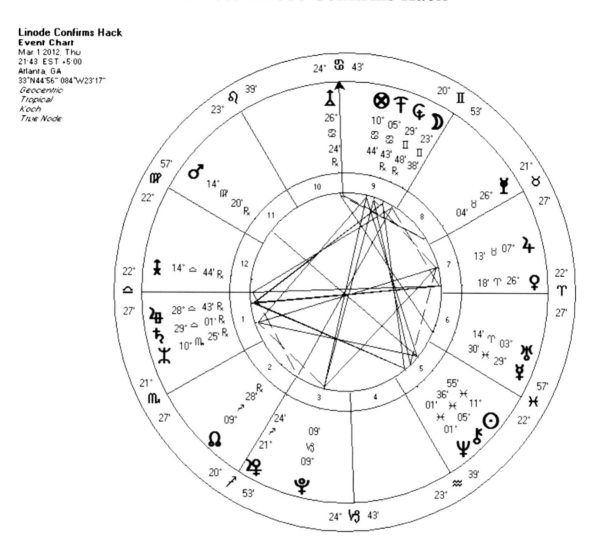

Linode Confirms Hack
Event Chart
Mar 1 2012, Thu
21:43 EST +5:00
Atlanta, GA
33°N44'56" 084°W23'17"
Geocentric
Tropical
Koch
True Node

Online bandits made off with more than 46,000 Bitcoin after exploiting a vulnerability in a widely-used web host that gave unfettered access to eight victims' digital wallets. The 46,703 stolen Bitcoin were worth about $228,845 at that time. More than 43,000 of the stolen BTC belonged to the Bitcoin trading platform Bitcoinica. Another 3,094 BTC were lifted from Marek Palatinus, a programmer from the Czech Republic. And Gavin Andresen, the lead Bitcoin programmer, reported that he had lost all five of the Bitcoin he had stored in one online account.

153

The Bitcoin Foundation

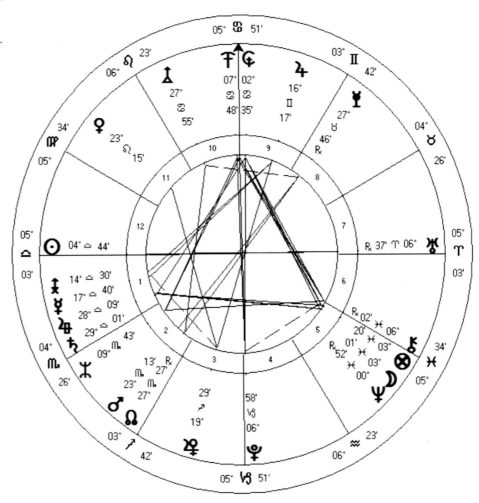

Bitcoin Foundation
Natal Chart
Sep 27 2012, Thu
06:55 EDT +4:00
New York, NY
40°N42'51" 074°W00'23"
Geocentric
Tropical
Koch
True Node

The Bitcoin Foundation was formed with the stated mission to "standardize, protect and promote the use of bitcoin cryptographic money for the benefit of users worldwide." According to its founding documents, the Bitcoin Foundation's original members included Gavin Andresen, Charlie Shrem, Mark Karpelès, Peter Vessenes, Roger Ver, Patrick Murck, Jon Matonis, and Mehul Puri. The timing for this chart is based on an article announcing the launch of the organization, written by board member Jon Matonis and published online at forbes.com.

WordPress Begins Accepting Bitcoin

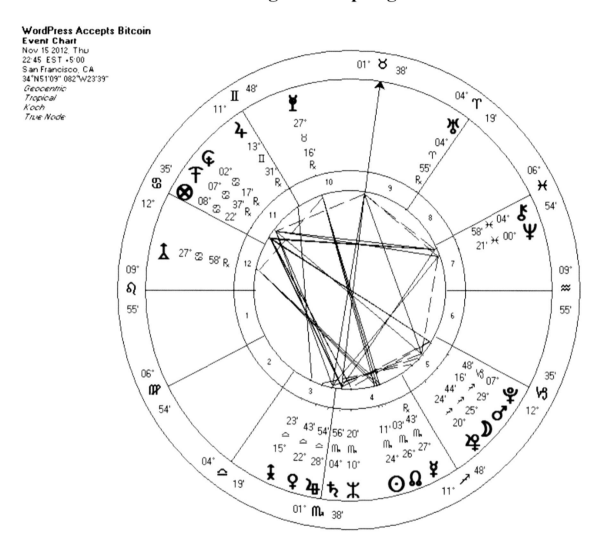

Andy Skelton, writing in the WordPress blog, announced that "you can now buy WordPress.com upgrades with bitcoins. PayPal alone blocks access from over 60 countries, and many credit card companies have similar restrictions. Some are blocked for political reasons, some because of higher fraud rates, and some for other financial reasons. Whatever the reason, we don't think an individual blogger from Haiti, Ethiopia, or Kenya should have diminished access to the blogosphere because of payment issues they can't control. Our goal is to enable people, not block them."

First Halving Day

First Halving Day
Event Chart
Nov 28 2012, Wed
15:24:38 UT +0:00
Greenwich, UK
51°N29' 000°W00'
Geocentric
Tropical
Koch
True Node

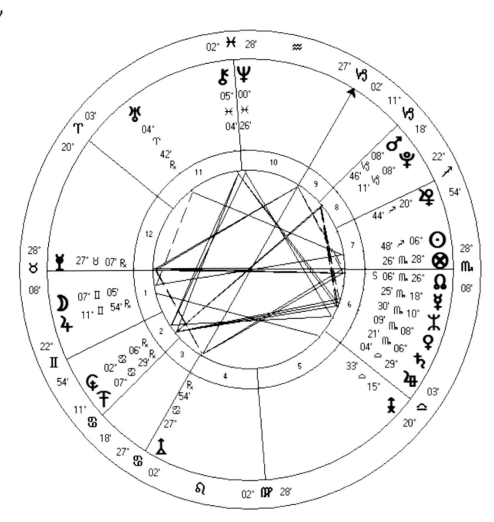

A press release from the Bitcoin Foundation announced a major milestone in the Bitcoin blockchain, marking the 210,000th block mined. On Halving Day, the reduction of the Bitcoin created per block reinforced the cryptocurrency's deflationary promise. For the first three years of the Bitcoin Network's existence, each time a block was found, 50 Bitcoins were issued to the lucky finder. As of block 210,000, however, only 25 Bitcoins were issued. Although Bitcoin miners began receiving less Bitcoin for each block mined, the decreased Bitcoin supply was expected to yield higher prices over time.

Cyprus Bailout Drives Bitcoin Higher

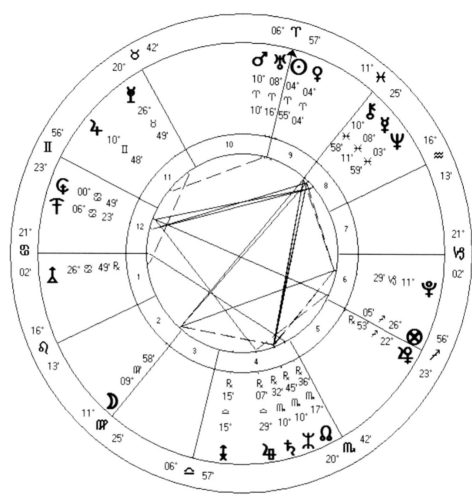

Cyprus Bailout Bitcoin Boom
Event Chart
Mar 25 2013, Mon
12:00 EET -2:00
Nicosia, Cyprus
35°N10' 033°E22'
Geocentric
Tropical
Koch
True Node

Orchestrated by Cyprus President Nicos Anastasiades, the Eurogroup, the European Commission, the ECB and the IMF, a €10 billion bailout was intended to rescue the flagging Cypriot economy. But one condition was a sizable levy collected from bank accounts worth over €100,000 – a big worry not just for wealthy Cypriots but for many internationals, since the country was a popular tax haven for Russians. Trying to preserve their assets before the plan took effect, large account holders began buying Bitcoin wildly, driving the value of one Bitcoin from about $80 to over $260 in just a few weeks.

Overloading The Mt. Gox Servers

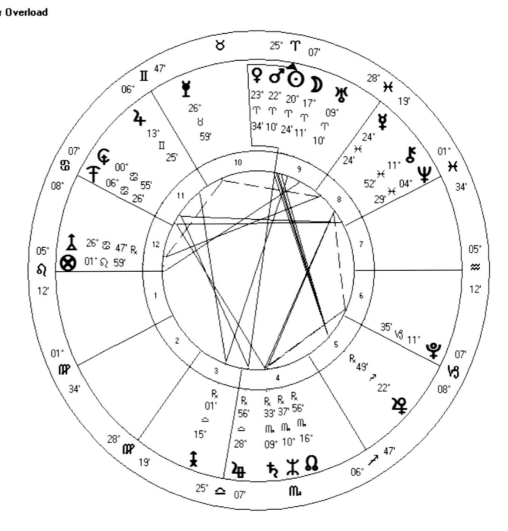

Thanks largely to the eager buying connected with the Cyprus bailout, the Mt. Gox Exchange reported that it had become a "victim of our own success!" Faced with a "rather astonishing amount of new accounts opened in the last few days added to the existing ones, plus the number of trades made," the firm's computers began to lag. "As expected in such a situation people started to panic, started to sell Bitcoin in mass (Panic Sale) resulting in an increase of trade that ultimately froze the trade engine!" The panic spread into the broader market and drove prices down sharply, before a recovery a few days later.

Ross Ulbricht Arrested in San Francisco

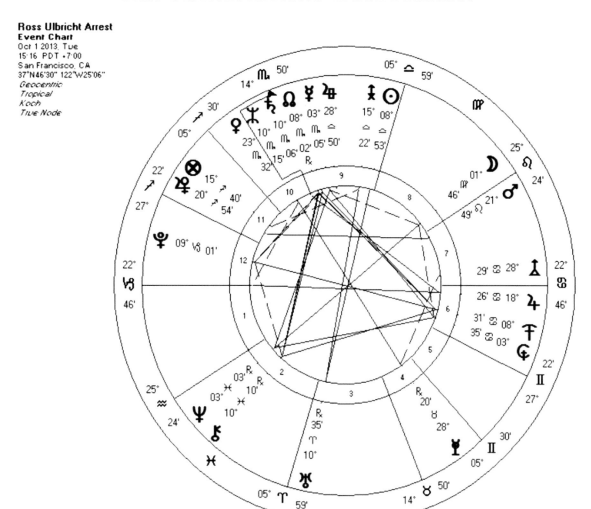

Ross Ulbricht Arrest
Event Chart
Oct 1 2013, Tue
15:16 PDT +7:00
San Francisco, CA
37°N46'30" 122°W25'06"
Geocentric
Tropical
Koch
True Node

Ross Ulbricht, the "Dread Pirate Roberts" who had created the notorious Silk Road website, was arrested at a public library after an extensive multi-state manhunt and federal sting operation. He was charged with narcotics trafficking, computer hacking, money laundering and engaging in a "continuing criminal enterprise." About 30,000 BTC of the Silk Road's alleged Bitcoin holdings are seized at the time, and an additional 144,000 BTC from Ulbricht's private holdings were confiscated three weeks later.

U.S. Senate Convenes A Hearing On Bitcoin

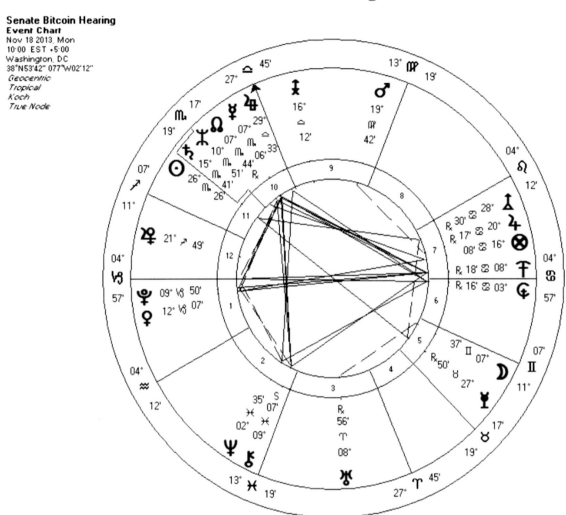

Senate Bitcoin Hearing
Event Chart
Nov 18 2013, Mon
10:00 EST +5:00
Washington, DC
38°N53'42" 077°W02'12"
Geocentric
Tropical
Koch
True Node

Coming just weeks after Ulbricht's arrest and announced under the title "Beyond Silk Road: Potential Risks, Threats, and Promises of Virtual Currencies," hope for the U.S. Government panel's discussion was dim among the Bitcoin community prior to the hearing. As the proceedings moved forward, however, many panelists and Senators agreed that Bitcoin holds great promise. The general consensus was summed up by Jennifer Shasky Calvery, Director of the U.S. Government's Financial Crimes Enforcement Network, who testified, "We want to operate in a way that does not hinder innovation."

China Declares That Bitcoin Is Not A Currency

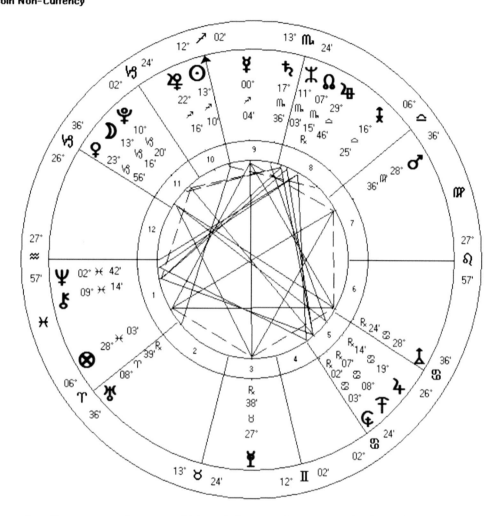

Putting its first restraints on Bitcoin's surging popularity, the People's Bank of China declares Bitcoin not to be a currency. Just two weeks earlier, the central Bank's vice governor Yi Gang had said "people are free to participate in the Bitcoin market," and that he would "personally adopt a long-term perspective on the currency." Trading volume at the largest Chinese Bitcoin exchange, BTC China, was already more than twice that of the world's second-largest exchange, Mt. Gox. The policy shift prohibited any financial institution to trade, insure, or otherwise offer services related to Bitcoin. Over the following weeks, Bitcoin prices around the globe began to sink dramatically.

Mt. Gox Exchange Closes

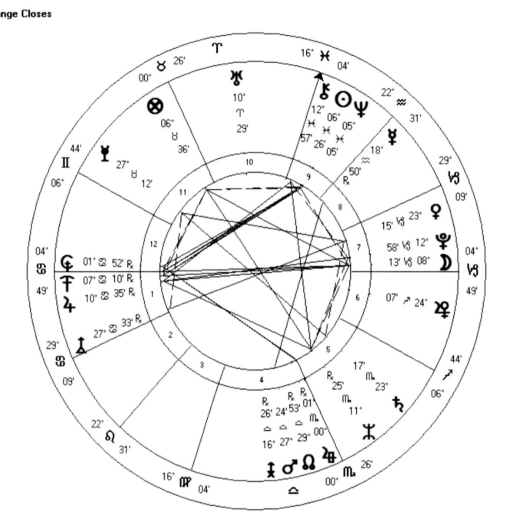

After putting an abrupt halt to withdrawals on February 6, claiming that a hacker had exploited their own poorly-implemented software through the use of transaction malleability attacks, disgraced bitcoin exchange Mt. Gox's website and trading engine went blank without official comment. Other exchanges and Bitcoin businesses issued a joint statement condemning the mismanagement, deception, and eventual collapse wrought by the executives of the Japan-based exchange, after an alleged leaked internal document showed that over 744,000 BTC were lost by the company.

IRS Sets Bitcoin Policy

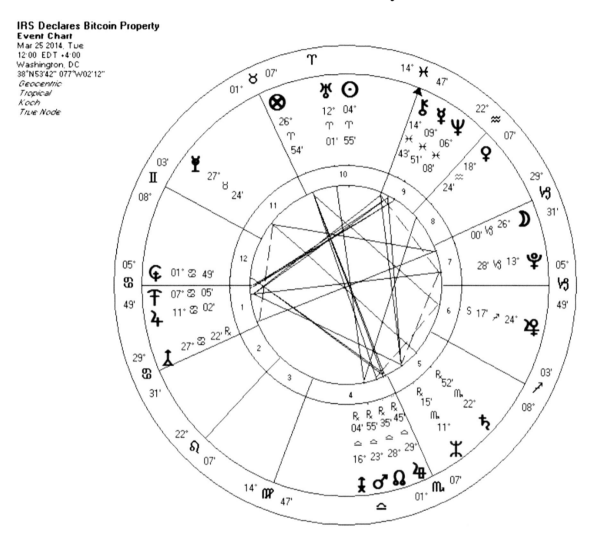

**IRS Declares Bitcoin Property
Event Chart**
Mar 25 2014, Tue
12:00 EDT +4:00
Washington, DC
38°N53'42" 077°W02'12"
*Geocentric
Tropical
Koch
True Node*

Following the lead of the People's Bank of China, an IRS policy document declared Bitcoin to be property, not currency, subject to capital gains tax calculated against every change in buying power for a given amount of Bitcoin, from the time it's acquired to the time it's spent. The stance was derided as unwieldy and overly complex, requiring a record of Bitcoin's market price with every transaction, subject to an array of unfamiliar calculations. While the net tax paid may be less than if Bitcoin were treated as currency proper, the move was not friendly to a market that emerged in tax-free innocence.

New York Proposes BitLicense

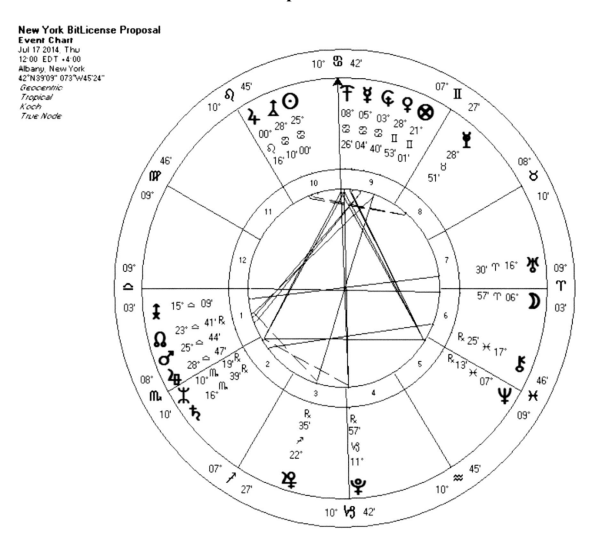

Benjamin M. Lawsky, Superintendent of New York's Department of Financial Services, proposed regulations for businesses using Bitcoin, to "protect consumers and root out illegal activity – without stifling beneficial innovation". The rules would require those who deal in Bitcoin to run background checks/fingerprints for all employees, get written state approval for any new business activities, and to convert any Bitcoin profit to US dollars. Affected businesses include ones based in New York state, or with customers there.

Bitcoin Market Slays The BearWhale

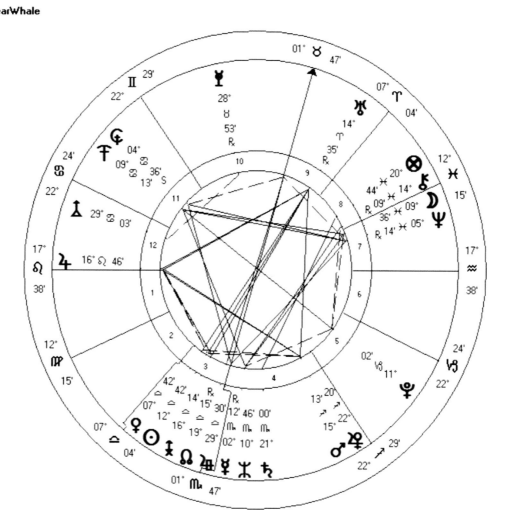

When someone posted a limit order in the early hours of Monday morning to sell 30,000 bitcoins at $300 each – well below the mid-300s price levels of trading throughout the weekend, the sheer size of the order spooked the market, sending prices plunging to levels not seen in more than a year. Bitcoin traders immediately named the seller "BearWhale," quickly spreading it through social media. And although he was eventually defeated – the entire order was cleared – Bitcoin enthusiasts mythologized the incident, creating artwork and poetry about the epic battle against this perceived bearishness.

Charlie Shrem Sentenced To Two Years In Prison

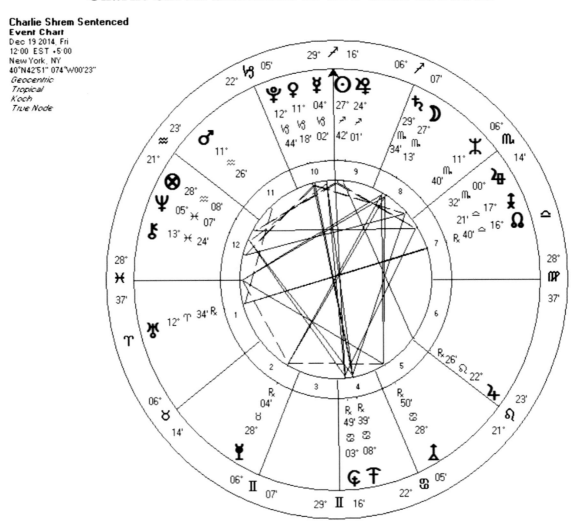

Labeled Bitcoin's "First Felon", 25-year-old Charlie Shrem, the CEO of bitcoin exchange BitInstant, was sentenced to 2 years in prison for his role in laundering money for users of the Silk Road online marketplace. Shrem had entered a plea bargain which involved surrendering $950,000 to the US government and pleading guilty to aiding and abetting the operation of an unlicensed money-transmitting business. "Considering I was facing 30 years, justice has been served," Shrem commented. "On a good note, Judge Rakoff called me a brilliant visionary and that he admires my brainpower."

Bitstamp Hack Results In $5 Million Loss

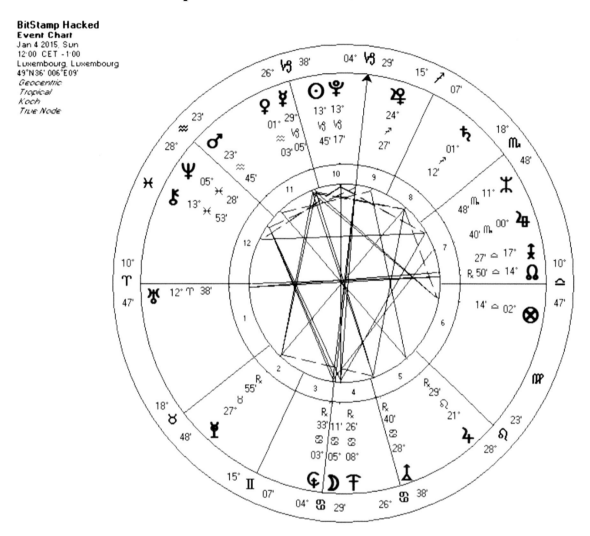

Following a hacking attack on Bitstamp, the company said that "On January 4th, some of Bitstamp's operational wallets were compromised, resulting in a loss of less than 19,000 BTC. Upon learning of the breach, we immediately notified all customers that they should no longer make deposits to previously issued bitcoin deposit addresses. As an additional security measure, we suspended our systems while we fully investigate the incident and actively engage with law enforcement officials." 19,000 Bitcoin was worth about $5.1 million at the time.

Ross Ulbricht Sentenced To Life Without Parole

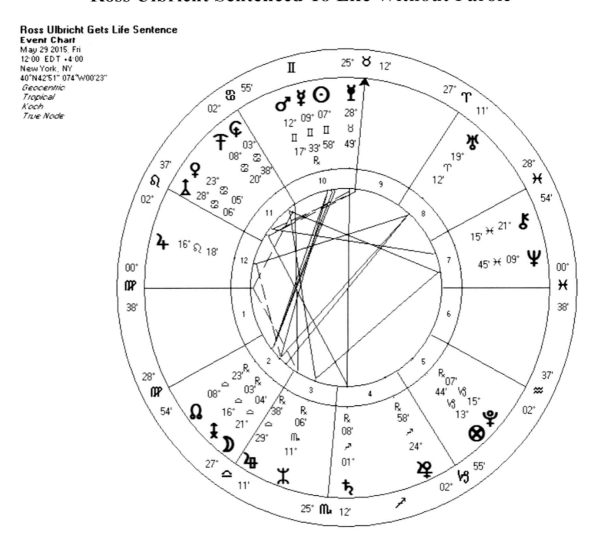

After a month-long jury trial that ended in Ross Ulbricht's conviction, Judge Katherine Forrest sentenced him to life in prison without parole. Ulbricht had been found guilty on 7 charges of money laundering, computer hacking, and conspiracy to traffic narcotics in February due to his role as the operator of the Silk Road marketplace. The judge's sentencing statement hinted that the harshness of the sentence was to make an example of Ulbricht: members of the public considering following in his footsteps should know "that if you break the law this way, there will be very serious consequences."

New York Releases BitLicense Regulations

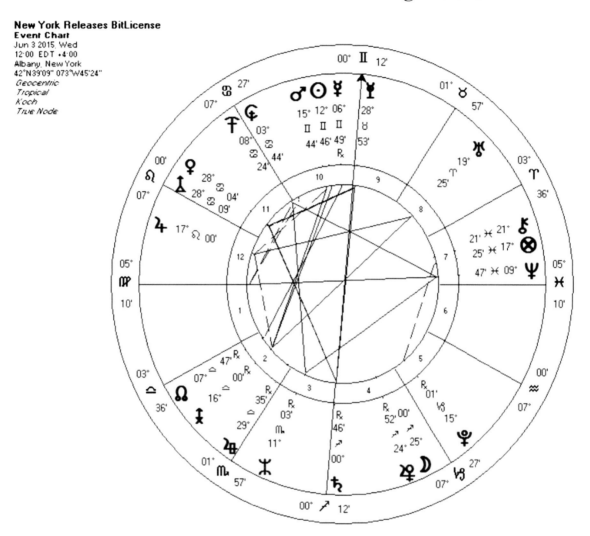

New York Releases BitLicense
Event Chart
Jun 3 2015, Wed
12:00 EDT +4:00
Albany, New York
42°N39'09" 073°W45'24"
Geocentric
Tropical
Koch
True Node

Superintendent of New York State Department of Financial Services Benjamin Lawsky, released a set of customized rules to regulate Bitcoin businesses that serve customers located in New York state. These regulations were the first ever directly to target digital currency businesses. They require companies that serve NY customers to apply for a "BitLicense" within 45 days or be considered in "breach of the law". A BitLicense application costs $5,000. In response, New York based customers were banned and expunged by Bitcoin companies including Bitfinex, Kraken, Bitquick.co, and ShapeShift.

Federal Agents Plead Guilty To Silk Road Theft

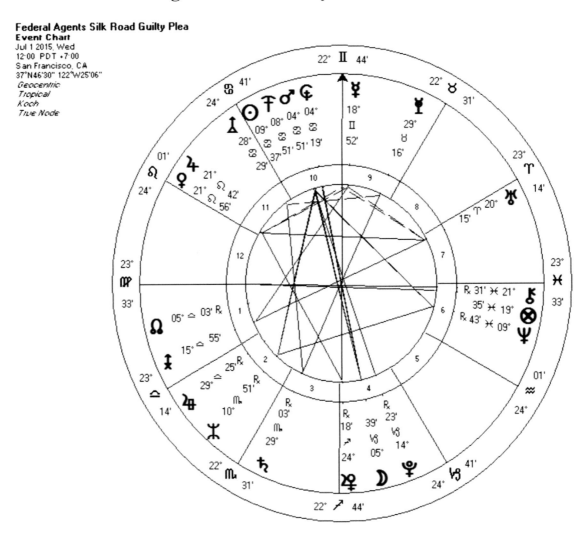

Federal Agents Silk Road Guilty Plea
Event Chart
Jul 1 2015, Wed
12:00 PDT +7:00
San Francisco, CA
37°N46'30" 122°W25'06"
Geocentric
Tropical
Koch
True Node

Former Federal agents Carl Force IV (DEA) and Shaun Bridges (Secret Service) pleaded guilty to stealing Bitcoins for personal gain during their investigation of the Silk Road marketplace. Force was charged with "extorting Ulbricht, as well as wire fraud, theft of government property, money laundering, and conflict of interest" in his role in siphoning off $50,000 worth of Bitcoin from the Silk Road into his own personal accounts. Bridges was charged with money laundering and obstruction of justice for stealing $820,000 worth of Bitcoin in a similar manner. Both men were given fines and prison terms.

Mark Karpelès Arrested In Tokyo

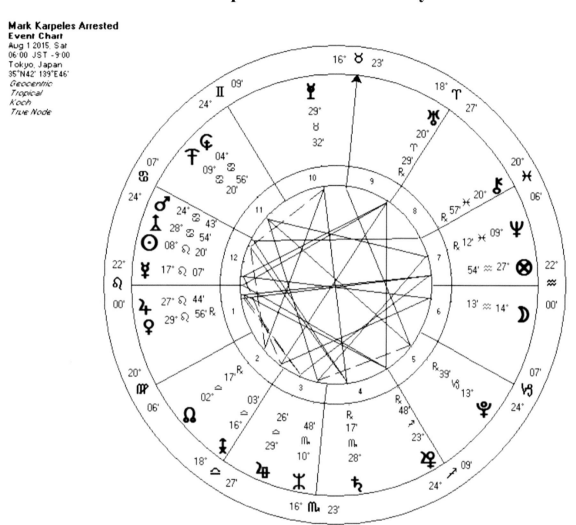

Mark Karpeles Arrested
Event Chart
Aug 1 2015, Sat
06:00 JST -9:00
Tokyo, Japan
35°N42' 139°E46'
Geocentric
Tropical
Koch
True Node

Police arrested Mt. Gox CEO Mark Karpelès in Japan on allegations that he manipulated volume on the then-market leading Bitcoin exchange platform prior to its 2014 collapse. The formal action from the Tokyo Metropolitan Police followed escalating reports that Karpelès was facing criminal charges for fraud and embezzlement. The arrest came more than a year after Mt. Gox first filed for bankruptcy protection in the US and Japan.

Gemini Bitcoin Exchange Opens

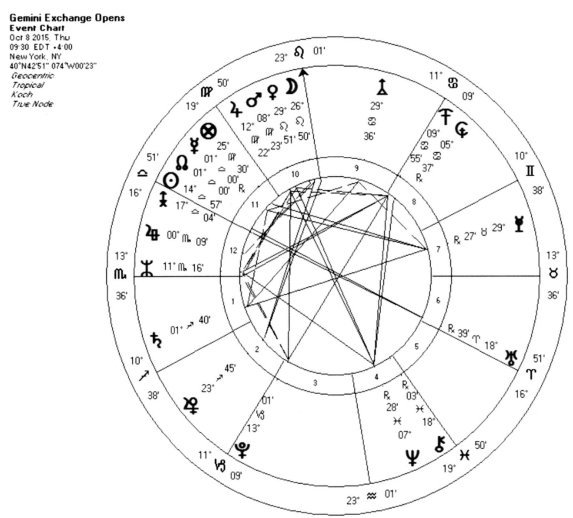

Gemini Exchange Opens
Event Chart
Oct 8 2015, Thu
09:30 EDT +4:00
New York, NY
40°N42'51" 074°W00'23"
Geocentric
Tropical
Koch
True Node

Cameron and Tyler Winklevoss released their own U.S.-based Bitcoin exchange dubbed "Gemini". Upon launch, the exchange was licensed to operate in 26 states and was able to "service both individual and institutional customers" due to its LLTC corporate structure. Gemini was also able to offer FDIC insurance on customer deposits, thanks to a partnership with a New York based bank. The exchange aims to be fully compliant with US law with a policy to first "ask for permission, not forgiveness".

Blockchain Featured By *Economist* Magazine

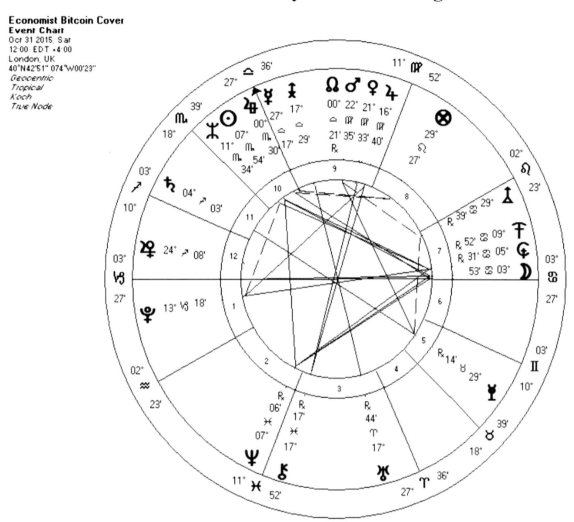

Economist Bitcoin Cover
Event Chart
Oct 31 2015, Sat
12:00 EDT +4:00
London, UK
40°N42'51" 074°W00'23"
Geocentric
Tropical
Koch
True Node

The Economist, a globally popular British publication focused on economic liberalism, made its article "The Trust Machine" the featured cover story of its weekly print edition. The article focused mainly on the utility of blockchain technology, promoting the idea that banks and government institutions may implement their own blockchains to create "cheap, tamper-proof public databases".

Standardized Bitcoin Sign Added To Unicode

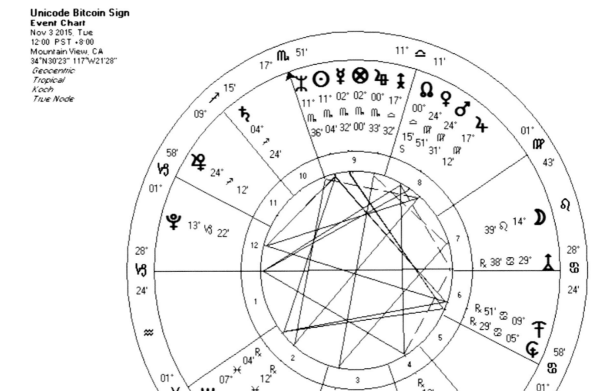

The Unicode committee accepted the Bitcoin currency symbol (uppercase B with 2 vertical bars going through it, but only visible at the top and bottom) to be in a future version of the Unicode standard. The glyph will be given the slot "U+20BF BITCOIN SIGN" and eventually will render with standard system fonts.

Bitcoin Roundtable Consensus

Bitcoin Roundtable Consensus
Event Chart
Feb 21 2016, Sun
12:00 AWST -8:00
Hong Kong, China
22°N17' 114°E09'
Geocentric
Tropical
Koch
True Node

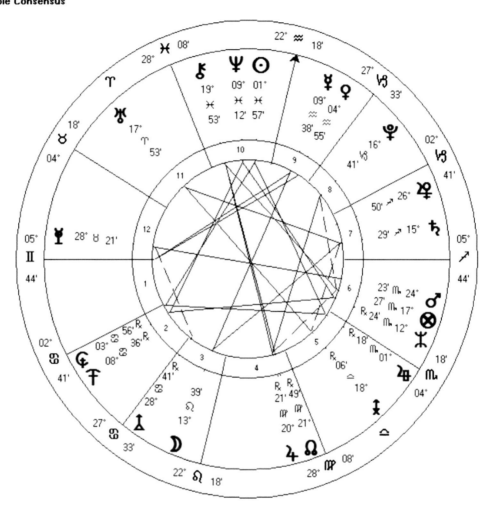

Influential members of the Bitcoin community held a closed-door meeting in Hong Kong to discuss a development plan and timeline for scaling Bitcoin and address solutions to the block size debate. The meeting ended with a public statement proposing the group's support for the new Segregated Witness functionality, and making a hard fork in the Bitcoin protocol available to the block size limit between 2MB and 4MB by July 2016. Others in the Bitcoin community denounced the meeting because the parties involved represented only a small handful of Bitcoin companies and special interest groups.

The Launch Of OpenBazaar

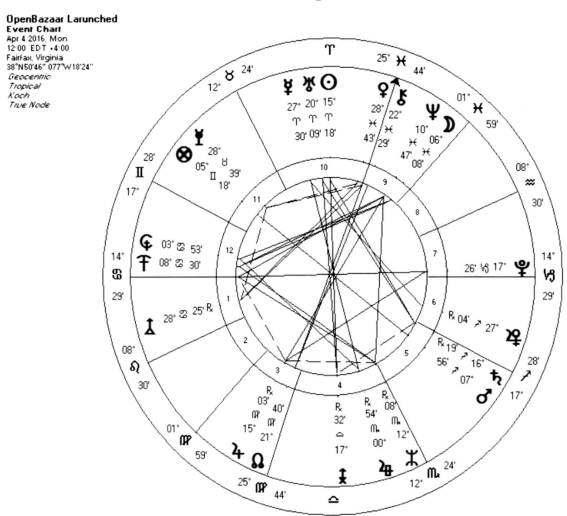

OpenBazaar Larunched
Event Chart
Apr 4 2016, Mon
12:00 EDT +4:00
Fairfax, Virginia
38°N50'46" 077°W18'24"
Geocentric
Tropical
Koch
True Node

The initial production version of the first decentralized marketplace software, OpenBazaar, was released to the general public. The goal of the OpenBazaar project was to facilitate peer-to-peer trade without a middleman, fees, or restrictions on trade. The software allows users to create virtual stores where buyers can purchase goods using Bitcoin. The OpenBazaar project would later announce it received $1 million in funding from venture capital firms Andreessen-Horowitz, Union Square Ventures, and angel investor William Mougayar.

Second Halving Day

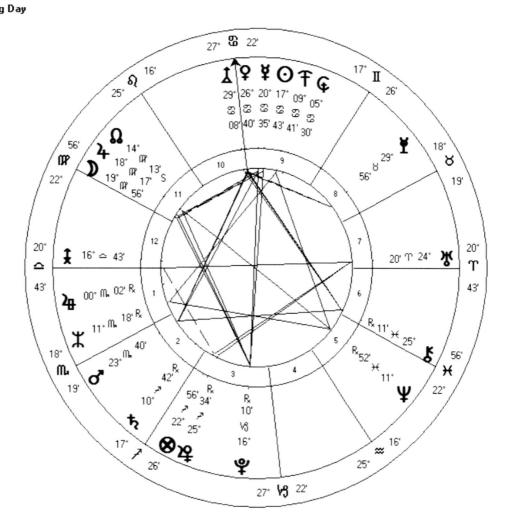

Although it was much anticipated within the Bitcoin community and discussed in the financial media as it approached, the Second Halving Day for Bitcoin mining eventually came and went without much noticeable impact on Bitcoin trading prices. Block 420,000 was mined on July 9, 2016. The miner listed in the ledger was Discus Fish. The reward payment for Block 420,000 was 12.5 BTC, compared with the 25.0 BTC payment for the previous block.

Winklevoss Bitcoin Trust ETF Authorization Denied

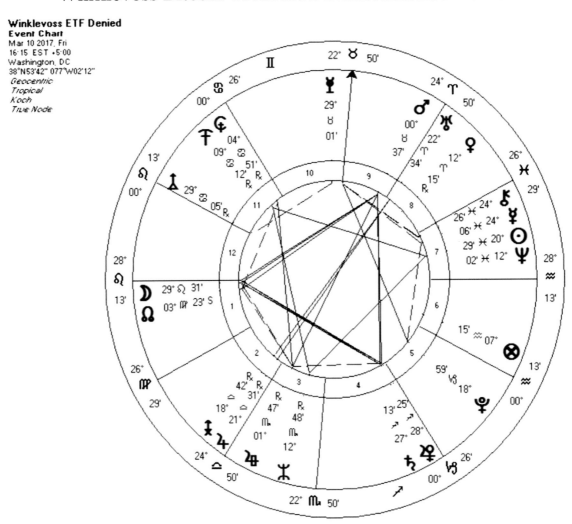

Winklevoss ETF Denied
Event Chart
Mar 10 2017, Fri
16:15 EST +5:00
Washington, DC
38°N53'42" 077°W02'12"
Geocentric
Tropical
Koch
True Node

The U.S. Securities and Exchange Commission denied the application of Tyler and Cameron Winklevoss – the twin brothers who once claimed to be co-inventors of Facebook – to operate an exchange-traded fund (ETF) to make it easier for investors to buy Bitcoin. The ruling torpedoed plans for the Winklevoss Bitcoin Trust, which currency investors had been closely watching. The price of Bitcoin dropped 14 percent, to about $1,022.68, immediately after the decision, which came shortly after the market closed.

Japan Declares Bitcoin Legal Tender

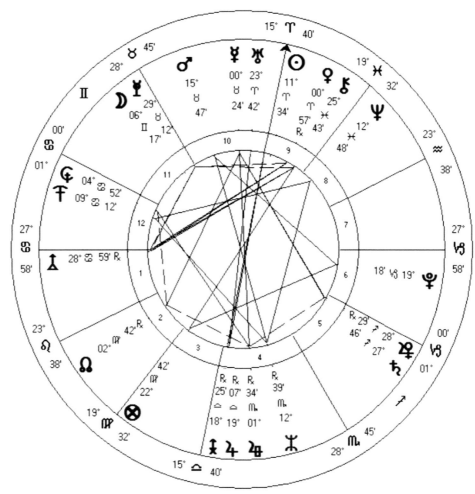

Bitcoin Legal Tender in Japan
Event Chart
Apr 1 2017, Sat
12:00 JST -9:00
Tokyo, Japan
35°N42' 139°E46'
Geocentric
Tropical
Koch
True Node

Japan recognizes Bitcoin as a legal and legitimate method of payment. Following months of animated debate, he country's legislature passed a law that brought Bitcoin exchanges under anti-money laundering/know-your-customer rules, while also categorizing Bitcoin as a kind of prepaid payment instrument.

Jamie Dimon Calls Bitcoin A Fraud

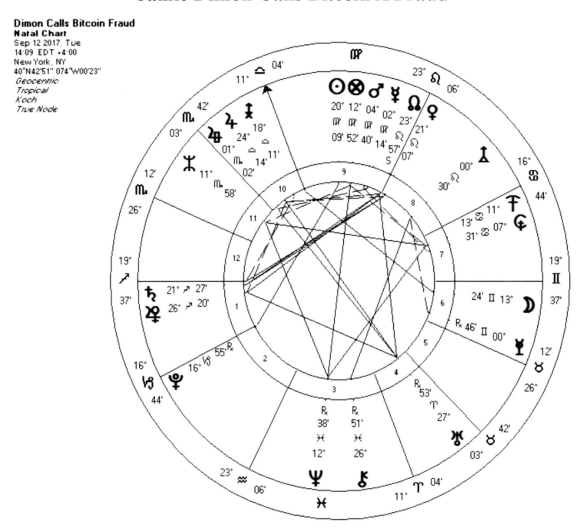

Dimon Calls Bitcoin Fraud
Natal Chart
Sep 12 2017, Tue
14:09 EDT +4:00
New York, NY
40°N42'51" 074°W00'23"
Geocentric
Tropical
Koch
True Node

JPMorgan Chase & Co. Chief Executive Officer Jamie Dimon said he would fire any employee of his company who was caught trading Bitcoin for being "stupid." The cryptocurrency "won't end well," he told an investor conference in New York, predicting it will eventually blow up. "It's a fraud" Dimon said, and "worse than tulip bulbs."

China Shuts Down Bitcoin Exchanges

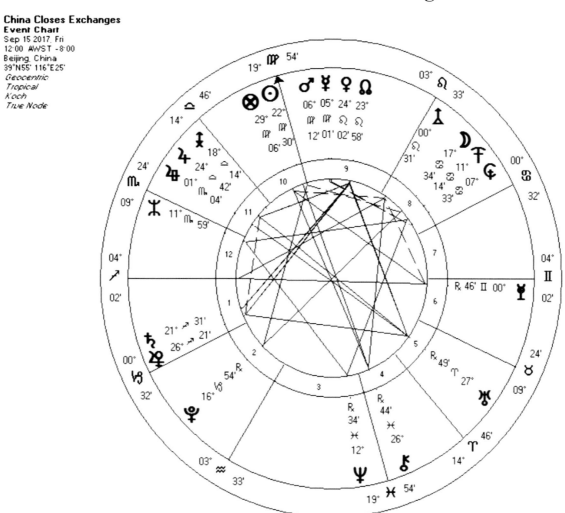

China Closes Exchanges
Event Chart
Sep 15 2017, Fri
12:00 AWST -8:00
Beijing, China
39°N55' 116°E25'
Geocentric
Tropical
Koch
True Node

Chinese authorities summarily ordered Beijing-based cryptocurrency exchanges to cease trading and immediately notify users of their closure, signaling a widening crackdown by the country's authorities on the industry, in an effort to contain financial risks. Exchanges were also told to stop allowing new user registrations, according to a government notice signed by the Beijing city group in charge of overseeing internet finance risks. The notice was circulated online and verified by a government source.

CME Announces Plans For Bitcoin Futures Trading

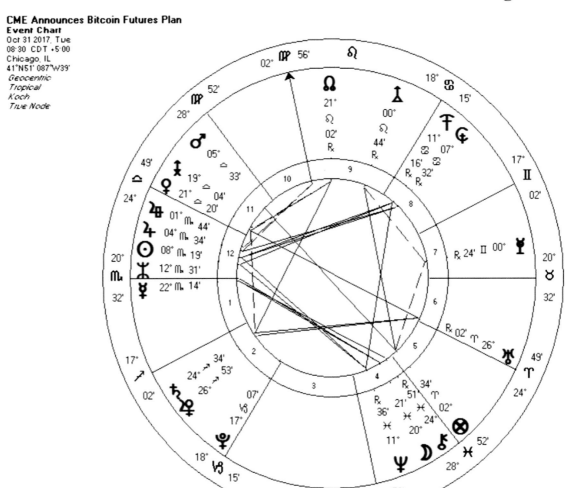

CME Group announced that it plans to introduce trading in Bitcoin futures by the end of the year, only a month after dismissing such a plan. Chief Executive Officer Terrence Duffy cited increased client demand as a key reason for the change of mind. As a result, the Bitcoin price hit a high of $6,600.84 just hours after breaking through the $6,400 barrier, and just one minute after moving past the $6,500 mark, according to data from Coin Desk. Its market capitalization, or the total value of Bitcoin in circulation, hit $110 billion.

Bitcoin Hits Record High Of $19,783.06

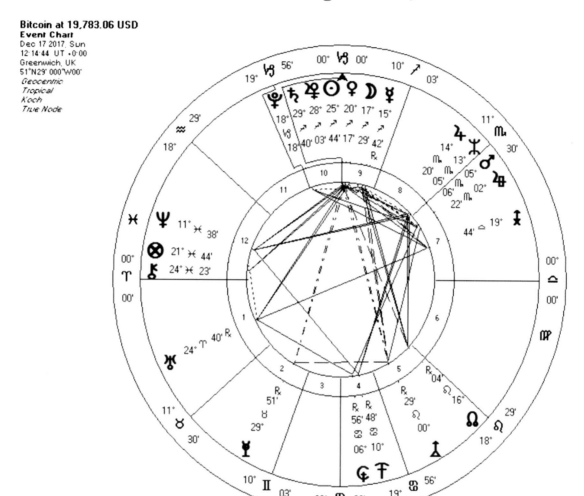

As recorded by Coin base, Bitcoin hit its all-time record high versus the US dollar at $19,783.06 at 12:14:44 UTC on December 17, 2017. As of May 1, 2018, this record still stands. While the event came just a couple of days before Saturn's ingress into Capricorn, what's noteworthy here is the extreme weakness of both Venus and Jupiter, the traditional money planets. Mars, on the other hand, is incredibly strong. It is both the ruler of the Ascendant and the final dispositor of the chart, and is also in its own sign, face and terms.

Mining Computer Theft Suspects Arraigned

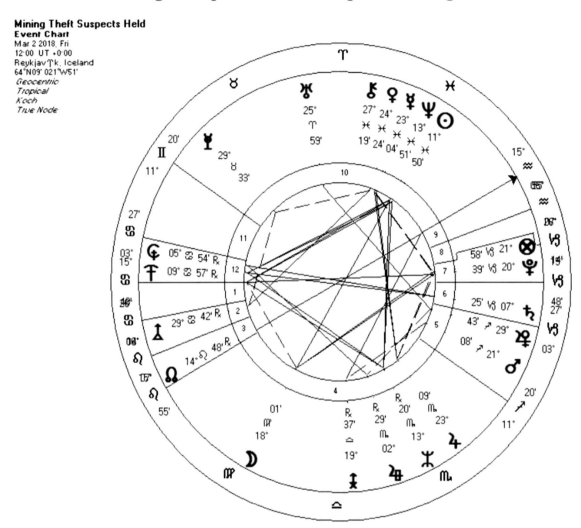

Some 600 computers used to mine Bitcoin and other virtual currencies were stolen from data centers in Iceland in what police said is the biggest series of thefts ever in the North Atlantic island nation. Eleven people were arrested, including a security guard, in what Icelandic media dubbed the "Big Bitcoin Heist." A judge at the Reykjavik District Court ordered two people to remain in custody. The powerful computers, which have not yet been found, are worth almost $2 million.

Dutch Court Upholds Bitcoin Claim

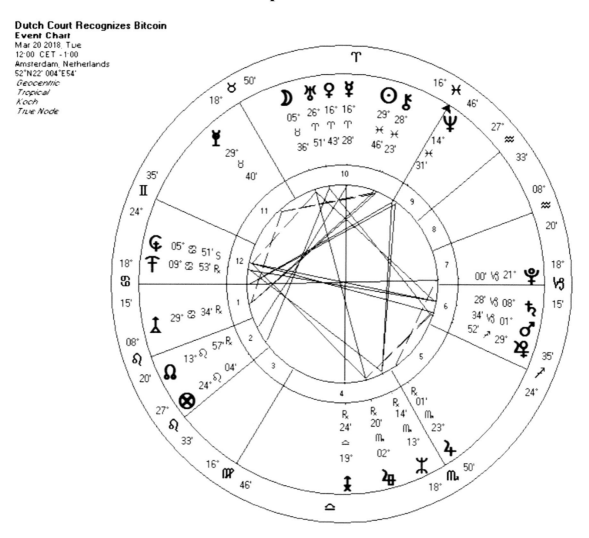

Dutch Court Recognizes Bitcoin
Event Chart
Mar 20 2018, Tue
12:00 CET -1:00
Amsterdam, Netherlands
52°N22' 004°E54'
Geocentric
Tropical
Koch
True Node

A court in the Netherlands ruled in favor of J. W. De Vries, who was owed 0.591 BTC by Koinz Trading, a crypto-mining company. The judgment called Bitcoin a "transferable value," which also means that it's legally usable. The court determined that Koinz Trading should pay their debt worth 0.591 BTC to de Vries. If not, the company will be fined €10,000 ($12,000USD). The Dutch court said it would declare the company bankrupt unless they paid the owed coins. The court ruled Bitcoin to be eligible for protection under the Property Rights Law.

Goldman Sachs Confirms Plans For Bitcoin Trading Desk

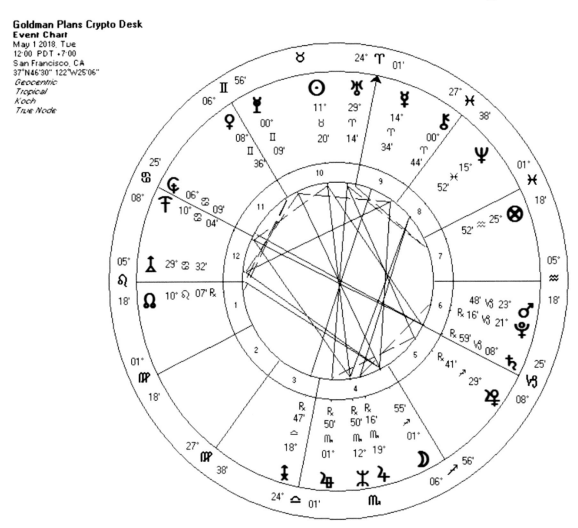

Goldman Plans Crypto Desk
Event Chart
May 1 2018, Tue
12:00 PDT +7:00
San Francisco, CA
37°N46'30" 122°W25'06"
Geocentric
Tropical
Koch
True Node

Investment banking giant Goldman Sachs confirmed that it is preparing to use its own funds to sponsor investment contracts tied to the Bitcoin price and hopes to eventually trade "physical Bitcoins" directly. The bank had denied rumors of the plan as recently as April 23, when it hired cryptocurrency trader Justin Schmidt, saying that it had "not reached a conclusion on the scope of our digital asset offering." But now the bank says it will begin offering clients non-deliverable forward contracts linked to Bitcoin, an asset that Goldman CEO Lloyd Blankfein has called a "vehicle to perpetrate fraud."

What Comes Next?

The horoscope charts we have shared here, and indeed this entire book on Bitcoin Astrology, is just the beginning. They tell a tale of fears and follies, of greed and altruism, and of fantasies and hope. But they also document important beginnings, and they make it clear that the story of Bitcoin is just getting started. In short, we anticipate adding many more horoscopes to this collection in the future.

As we move through an intense period of planetary transformation between 2018 and 2022, and then into the years beyond, we are on the cusp of a new consciousness that will create fresh concepts and definitions of who we truly are as individuals, as communities, and as a planet. Our mission is to become intentional co-creators of that transformation, no matter what our personal backgrounds, beliefs, or resources may be.

This ongoing process calls upon us to combine an empathetic understanding of shared human experience with the latest rapid-fire innovations in technology, and with astrology's most sacred spiritual and alchemical roots.

The ultimate role that Bitcoin and its progeny will play in that ever-changing amalgamation remains to be seen. But if we willingly embrace this unique opportunity by using Bitcoin and other cryptocurrencies in our personal commerce, and by actively creating innovative economic models for meaningful transactions, we are likely to be amazed.

That amazement – that profound sense of wonder – can open up boundless new personal possibilities for us. It can also become a steady fire for the alembic of even greater transmutations to come.

Additional Resources

http://astrocryptoconnection.com

www.billmeridian.com

https://financialcyclesweekly.com

www.financialuniverse.co.uk

https://www.fxstreet.com

www.wendystacey.com

Made in the USA
Lexington, KY
10 May 2018